DISCOVERING SHAKESPEARE

A Chapter in Literary History

A.L.Rowse

Weidenfeld and Nicolson
London

Copyright © A. L. Rowse, 1989

First published in Great Britain by
George Weidenfeld and Nicolson Ltd
91 Clapham High Street, London SW4 7TA

Printed in Great Britain at The Bath Press, Avon

British Library Cataloguing in Publication Data
Rowse, A.L. (Alfred Leslie), 1903–
   Discovering Shakespeare.
   1. Drama in English. Shakespeare, William, 1564–1616
   I. Title
   822.3′ 3
   ISBN 0–297–79633–X

*This book is dedicated to
My Readers*

Contents

Preface   ix

1   The Historian's Approach   1
2   Shakespeare's Autobiography   14
3   The Discovery of the Dark Lady   32
4   New Light on the Early Plays   60
5   The History Plays and Contemporary Life   80
6   Light on the Later Plays   102
7   *The Contemporary Shakespeare*   129
8   Criticism   146
9   'Experts' and Media-men   158

Index   173

Preface

It is now a quarter of a century since I began my intensive work on William Shakespeare, beginning properly with the life of the man. Before that I had devoted another quarter of a century to research into the Elizabethan age, the necessary background to his life and work. Without that people cannot be expected to get it right – as most of them do not.

The long trail has led to many discoveries, some of them – like the discovery of the Dark Lady, in the Bodleian at Oxford – quite unexpected. If my previous working out of the solutions to the problems of the Sonnets had not been entirely correct, I should not have had that bonus. It was a reward for sticking to my findings: it confirmed them, they corroborated each other.

Indeed, it was an initial surprise that the so-called problems of the Sonnets should have worked out consistently and intelligibly, once I got down to them. They never had been solved before, they had been subject to endless confusion and worthless conjectures. 'What a mess they have made of it!' Harold Macmillan wrote. They needed an Elizabethan historian to clear up the mess, who could lay the firm foundation of dating and explaining the topical references. What is a historian for? In fact a firm foundation could not be laid without one, and this was the first time that an Elizabethan historian had devoted himself to them.

So it should not have been so very surprising that he was successful in solving them.

The reaction of the Shakespeare Establishment – perhaps one should say 'Industry', or 'Trade Union' – was no less a surprise to me. So far from being grateful for having their problems solved for them they greeted my work at first with incomprehension, then gathered themselves together to obstruct, and confuse the public further. It did not give them any pleasure that the public, more open-minded, particularly in America – which had no vested interest in keeping the confusion going – were more generous and welcomed my findings.

That merely added envy to obtuseness and stupidity. They had not even the tactical sense to see that the discoveries of the leading historian of Shakespeare's age offered a first line of defence against all the nonsense with which the subject is littered, and from which they themselves suffer. From the beginning I warned them that the confusion in which they left the subject opened the gate for all the crackpots to canter through. They could not even see that; they took no notice, but went on in their conventional way – in the old well-worn rut.

It makes a highly discreditable story, and I have always intended to tell it. Not only for its own interest as a significant chapter in literary history – it has a sociological aspect, with a salutary message for our time. I doubt if it would have happened before the dividing line of the Second World War, in a society where people still knew their place and could recognise quality when they saw it. Confusion of standards, intellectual and artistic – or absence of them – is endemic, like a disease, in contemporary society.

The trade union aspect of my story is this: the Eng. Lit. people thought of me as an historian trespassing in their field. There is a certain difference of approach which we can observe here. An Eng. Lit. writer is given to conjectures, and often cannot see the difference between a conjecture and historical fact, will even prefer the former. For example, it is absurd to give currency to the entirely modern invention that Marlowe was assassinated; when the coroner's inquest tells us specifically that he was killed accidentally in a quarrel over 'le reckoning', and Shakespeare concurs – he knew.

Or again there is their propensity for resurrecting scraps of inferior verse, as if they were Shakespeare's – while neglecting what we *can* learn from proper historical method applied consistently all through the work. Perhaps they fight shy of that since they know so little history; some of them, as we shall see, are positively hostile to it.

But they should *learn*, as I learn from good literary scholars, like Professor C.J.Sisson, for example. Since they have so far refused to learn, in this book I am telling them.

Here I have an advantage they did not perceive. I have always been equally devoted to history *and* literature – and have made full use of this advantageous ambivalence. In fact I was writing poetry for years before I had dared to venture on a work of historical research, and have continued writing verse all my life. At Oxford I was originally intended for literature, with an Eng. Lit. scholarship at Christ Church, where the dons made me take the History School, a better and more exacting School, a more solid intellectual foundation for future work. In my initial work on Shakespeare it was a practical advantage to be working in the Huntington Library (originally dedicated to the English Renaissance) where History and Literature were equally accessible on open shelves.

Some of the trouble arises from the over-specialisation of our time, indeed the compartmentation – where I am a believer in the cross-fertilisation of disciplines, unimaginatively held apart. While Eng. Lit. people are insufficiently read in history, many historians are insufficiently read in literature, though they are not so foolish as to be hostile. Once in USA, when I informed a history class of the existence of Robert Lowell's 'The Quaker Graveyard at Nantucket', finest of modern American poems, an innocent youth piped up, 'you should be in the Literature Department'. One might compare this with the junior lecturer at McGill, who told Hugh MacLennan that he did not read my Shakespeare books: 'you see, he is not *in the field*'.

In a democratic society it is a duty to give these people their proper rating: how otherwise can they learn?

I am sometimes asked if my views are 'accepted'. Accepted by whom? By people who could not tell what is right from wrong? It is not just a question of *nil admirari* – though Sainte Beuve tells us, 'Le *nil admirari* en effet n'est pas une marque d'intelligence.' The real mark of intelligence is to be able to tell, sooner rather than later.

My companion at arms in the campaign for commonsense about Shakespeare writes: 'I don't think you need worry about *public* appreciation of your work on Shakespeare – and even the Shakespeare industry is gradually changing its mind, under the weight of evidence. The Eng. Lit. professors are beginning to say, in private of course, that Emilia *is* the Dark Lady: eventually they will accept it publicly.' Here is a contrast with the historical profession, only too glad to welcome new knowledge based on irrefutable evidence.

He continues: 'I have often wondered *why* the Shakespeare establishment is to stupid and narrow, and, like you, have thought of writing something on it. I'm sure that personal envy plays a part; there is also the jealous exclusiveness of the narrow-minded. But above all there is the fear that biography and historical fact will somehow spoil literary criticism. They must have the "freedom" to do what they like with Shakespeare – any interpretation, however silly, except the topical and right one.'

I fear that this also is true, when one considers the reception they accord to nonsensical interpretations of every kind – anything rather than historical commonsense from the leading historian of the age. And of course they would be incapable of appreciating that however new and illuminating my discoveries and findings my approach is fundamentally traditional, confirming the tradition, and even cautious. I would never make a mistake like that about Marlowe, or with the inferior verse they would impute to Shakespeare.

To conclude: 'There is also the typical view of the narrow scholar that "the artist" is somehow remote from the world, and has nothing to do with daily life. This is a pernicious reversal of the truth. The artist, unlike the literary critic, is involved in life. But they want Shakespeare to be as narrow as themselves. I really don't worry about them any more – they are worth nothing.'

This is a drastic judgment on them, coming from one of their own profession. Cautious Cornishman as I am, I hardly like to go as far as a recent writer in the *Times Literary Supplement*: 'the time has come to wonder whether we can dispense with academic criticism in literary biographies entirely'.

I repeat that I have written this book for the information of the general reader; in my view it tells a shocking story.

For my own part it is a pleasure to acknowledge my indebtedness for many happy years of research: above all to All Souls and the Bodleian Library at Oxford, and to the Huntington Library in California. Also to a number of university libraries in the United States, to the London Library and that of the Athenaeum, and to the old Public Record Office in Chancery Lane, of nostalgic memory.

A friend assures me that at the very least it is convenient to have mention of my various Elizabethan discoveries, historical and literary, brought together within the covers of one book.

A.L.R.

1

The Historian's Approach

When Dr William Harvey, greatest of English physiologists, first discovered the circulation of the blood, nobody would credit it, and his practice – though he was the leading doctor of the time – fell away markedly. This is how it is with ordinary conventional minds: they cannot take in a new idea, let alone a discovery that upsets their preconceived notions, that they were brought up in, unless and until it is rubbed in to them. And not even then: very often one has to wait until a younger generation grows up that can absorb the new knowledge and acclimatise itself to it, leaving the obscurantists behind, where they were.

This was the case with the genius of a scientist, as John Aubrey tells us. 'I have heard him say that, after his book of the Circulation of the Blood came out, he fell mightily in his practice. And that 'twas believed by all the vulgar that he was crack-brained; all the physicians were against his opinion and envied him. Many wrote against him. With much ado at last, in about 20 or 30 years time, it was received in all the universities. And, as Mr Hobbes says, "he is the only man, perhaps, that ever lived to see his own doctrine established in his lifetime".'[1]

Harvey had to live to a good age in order to see this happy consummation; his view of the matter was bound to prevail in the end, for it was correct – not that of the conventional third-rate who could not even take it in when it was pointed out to them. They had nothing

---

[1] John Aubrey, *Brief Lives*, ed. A.Clark, I. 300–01.

to urge against it, for it was in fact unanswerable. More than that: his view not only set the matter right, explained things that had remained in confusion before – problems 'insoluble' to ordinary minds – but pointed the way to the future: to an immense extension of knowledge that followed from it.

I have had a similar experience with my discoveries about Shakespeare, my reduction of the so-called 'problems' to common sense. My settlement of the dating of the Sonnets, their character, to and for whom they were written, the identity of the rival poet and Shakespeare's mistress, the dark young lady; the obvious dedication by the publisher, not by Shakespeare, to 'Mr W.H.', who had got the manuscript. There followed upon this firm basis – as it certainly would not have done had it not all been correct from the first – any number of further discoveries regarding the Plays. In particular the entirely autobiographical character of *The Two Gentlemen of Verona*, similarly with *Love's Labour's Lost* with its intimate relation to the circle of young Southampton, Shakespeare's patron, when previously it had been thought insolubly enigmatic. There followed the settlement of the date and occasion of *A Midsummer Night's Dream*, with further light on the background of other plays, *All's Well That Ends Well, Coriolanus, Timon of Athens* and, more pointedly, *Cymbeline* and *Henry VIII*.

All this was too much to be absorbed in one gulp, for it revolutionised our knowledge of our greatest writer, turned him from a two-dimensional, somewhat indefinite figure open to all sorts of nonsense conjectures, into a three-dimensional one about whom there was a good deal of firm, irrefutable information.

For several reasons this ought not to be surprising, or to have left people merely annoyed, though incapable of answer as it did. In the first place it is in keeping with William Shakespeare's own nature. Ben Jonson, who knew him well, tells us: 'he was indeed honest [in Elizabethan English this meant honourable, a person of honour], and of an open free nature.'[1] That means that there was nothing mysterious about him. We know that he was prudent and tactful, above all a gentleman – unlike some other denizens of the theatre world. Though he was rather up-stage and emphasised his gentility (as Congreve and Pope did later) his nature was *open*. He

---

[1] q. E.K.Chambers, *William Shakespeare*, II. 210.

did not write the Sonnets to create a mystery: they were all too auto-biographical, too near the bone. That is why he did not publish them: they were not published until years after they were written, and then by an interesting, and interested, publisher who got the manuscript from *his* – not Shakespeare's – Mr W.H.

For a second reason: most people suppose – and people go on repeating it who should learn better – that we do not know much about our greatest writer. The truth is quite otherwise: we know more about him than about any other Elizabethan dramatist, except for the *later* life of Ben Jonson (we know far less about Ben's earlier life). In the Elizabethan age it was not the thing to bother about the lives of theatre folk, or even writers, unless they were grandees like Philip Sidney, or voluble clerics. About most of the dramatists we know very little – about Ford, Webster, Tourneur, Massinger, Middleton etc – but we know a lot about Shakespeare. We have a great deal of information about his family in Stratford, where his father was an alderman, as also about the whole Stratford and Warwickshire background. And for another thing, for the very reason that so much of Shakespeare's early work was *autobiographical*, that he put so much of himself and his experience to date into it. That is why it is so *living*, when most Elizabethan dramatists are rather dead; after all, he was the only one of them to write an autobiography – in the Sonnets. And yet there have been dumb academics writing about the Sonnets as mere literary 'exercises'! With such lack of perception such people ought not to be writing about the subject, and the reader can ignore most of what they write about it and him.

Finally, to know all this, to understand and interpret it, let alone the subtler business of correctly assessing judgments and values, an *intimate* knowledge of the Elizabethan age and society is essential. Very few people even among Shakespeare 'scholars' possess that, and so lack an indispensable qualification. Hence it is hardly surpris-ing that they get so many things wrong, irritating as it is when they do not realise it, get the life of our greatest writer all wrong, needlessly mislead people, and open the gate to every kind of conjectural non-sense.

So it was odd that people were vexed that the so-called 'problems' were settled for them, reduced to common sense, by a foremost auth-ority on Shakespeare's age and time. I wonder why? Someone said that it was like taking away a bone from a dog. For the moment it is enough to say that they preferred not to be disturbed and to go on in the old ruts that the conventional prefer – an easier life for them.

Not all, however. In one way I was rather luckier than Harvey, for two of the leading people in the English Literature School at Oxford saw the point of my discoveries, one of them at once, the other rather later.

The *doyen* of Shakespeare studies at Oxford at the time was Professor F.P.Wilson, a cautious scholar of sound judgment, who took no risks. He was the only person to whom I confided the fact – by letter from the Huntington Library where I did the initial work – that to my surprise *all* the so-called problems of the Sonnets had worked out straightforwardly, with the exception of the identity of the young dark mistress. *That* I thought then we should never discover.

F.P.Wilson wrote back to me, 'your news is indeed startling. You say that my first reaction will be surprise and scepticism that it should have been left to you to make the discovery. My first reaction was indeed surprise and scepticism *not* that the discovery should have been made by you. If Hotson had written to me in those terms I should have said to myself "another mare's nest". He told me a few years ago that he had discovered who Mr W.H. was. He has not published yet, but when he does I known I shan't believe him. But when *you* tell me, that is another matter altogether, especially as you have found the answer by historical evidence. I have often envied your knowledge of the nobility and gentry of the Elizabethan age, their houses and their marriages, their characters and intrigues; so if the problem was to be solved, who more likely to do so than you?' I asked him to keep the discovery private, and promised to read him the crucial chapters of my book when I got back to Oxford.

He came down from Cumnor to my rooms at All Souls, and at the end of the reading said, in his slow deliberate way: 'I can only say that I am deeply impressed, and have nothing whatever to urge against it.' We then went on to discuss the light that this threw on the supposed 'enigma' of *Love's Labour's Lost*, where Wilson had a good point to make. He was already in his last illness and shortly died: a loss to scholarship, and a sad loss to me in my campaign for common sense about Shakespeare.

Professor Nevill Coghill was less of a scholar, but he had a touch of genius as a producer of plays. His production of *The Tempest* in the garden of Worcester College, with the background of the lake, was one of the most moving I have ever seen. It was not long after the ending of the Second War the Germans had inflicted on Europe: there were the young men, survivors, back from various fronts. At the end, when Ariel tripped across the water to say farewell to Prospero's barge moving away down the lake, and the moon rose behind the trees, one's heart turned over.[1]

At first Nevill did not grasp the significance of the fact that Mr W.H., of Thorp's dedication of the Sonnets, was just Thorp's dedicatee and not Shakespeare's young lord *inside* the Sonnets. A year or two later he came up to me in Merton Street – I can see him now, at the corner of the Corpus building – and announced to me with enthusiasm that Mr W.H. was not Shakespeare's man at all. For once I did not say 'I told you so', pleased that he had seen the light at last. It is indeed the key that unlocks the sense of the Sonnets.

Most people still do not see what is indeed completely obvious and undeniable. Thorp signs the dedication to 'the only begetter', W.H., the one and only man who had got the manuscript. It is natural enough that ordinary people have not even yet got the point – as Henry James says: 'Nobody ever understands *anything*.' I don't blame them: I blame the people whose duty it is to tell them, the professors, the academics, teachers, the literary papers and periodicals, the media. Naturally even the reference books go on with the same old confusion: the up-to-date, revised edition of *Chambers' Biographical Dictionary* still reads, 'the favourite guess is that the young man – "Mr W.H." is Henry Wriothesley, Earl of Southampton, to whom the poems were dedicated; but it may be William Herbert, Earl of Pembroke, the lover of Mary Fitton who is not "the Dark Lady of the Sonnets", since she was fair.'

You see what a muddle this is, reader. That writer has got as far as to see that Mary Fitton could never have been the 'Dark Lady', because she was not dark. Actually, from her portraits at Arbury, she was auburn, rather than fair. But the real point is that her affair with Pembroke took place in 1600, years later than the Sonnets,

---

[1] Because Coghill was a first-rate producer the second-rate at Oxford kept him out of producing as much as they could. They are forgotten, his memory remains.

which were written from 1591 to 1594.[1] Non-historians hardly ever know how decisive dates are. Notice again the muddle in saying that the Sonnets were dedicated to Southampton: they are *not* – they were all about Southampton, written to and for him, but dedicated by Thorp to another person, someone close to Southampton, whose initials were WH – when Southampton's of course were HW. I saw this from the first, when I got down to the supposedly insoluble problem. 'The problem of the Sonnets is insoluble' summed up the attitude of ordinary academics; therefore, when it was solved for them, so far from being grateful, they were annoyed. Why? – didn't they want to know? Evidently not.

Agatha Christie – who was a good Shakespearean as well as having a sharp detective mind – gives us the secret when she writes: 'People always overlook the significance of the obvious.' They miss what is right under their noses. We have to rub their noses in it: Mr W.H. was Thorp's man, to whom he expressed his gratitude in his usual flowery language. Agatha had no difficulty in grasping the significance of this, and wrote to me charmingly as 'the mistress of low-brow detection to the master of high-brow detection.' I did not think of myself as such: I was just an historical scholar working out problems in an historian's common sense fashion.

But if I had not got all the answers correct – particularly the dating and proper sequence of events, plays, ages of the persons involved, etc – I might never have made the later discoveries, in particular the identity of the Dark Lady. That discovery was a bonus for sticking to my guns, in spite of incomprehension and obstruction. Fortunately a lifetime's experience has taught me to take no notice of what people think; most people do not know how to *think*, strictly speaking. Then it is our duty, especially in an egalitarian society, in which people suppose themselves to know when they do not, for those who *do* to tell them. In this duty the intellectuals have mostly betrayed their function – as in so many other respects, notably regarding politics and society, as people increasingly realise.[2] So this literary investigation will have its sociological aspects.

I was not looking for the Dark Lady when, to my astonishment,

---

[1] For her interesting and wayward career v. 'The True Story of Mary Fitton', in my *Discoveries and Reviews*.
[2] cf. Paul Johnson, *Intellectuals*.

she turned up – in the very place she would be, if anywhere, in the Bodleian Library among the papers and case-books of Simon Forman. Hundreds of Elizabethans, from the top of society to the bottom, came to consult him, medically and astrologically. To know who they all were one needed a comprehensive knowledge of who was who at the time. Already Forman had his importance for Shakespeare studies, for his account of seeing three or four of his plays at the Globe in 1611 was well known, and had been reprinted by E.K. Chambers and others. But Chambers had not delved any deeper into Forman's manuscripts. I went into them in depth and in detail – at two periods after an interval of some years: not because I was looking for any Dark Lady, but for the portrait of society I was depicting in my *Elizabethan Renaissance: The Life of the Society*.

Forman was acquainted with the family of Lord Hunsdon, Patron of Shakespeare's Company; he had known Hunsdon's son, the second Lord, over years, whose sister Margaret, Lady Hoby, was also a client of Forman's. Lo, and behold, there turned up another in that close circle: the old Lord's discarded mistress, Emilia Bassano, young Mrs Lanier, half-Italian, daughter of one of the Queen's musicians, married off to another; the very characteristics, circumstances, age etc. to corroborate with the unmistakable detailed portrait of her in the Sonnets. Much more was to emerge about her from further research – every fact consistently confirming and corroborative, and *not one single fact to the contrary*. That to an historian gives certainty.

This time Coghill saw the point at once. He wrote to me: 'Your Dark Lady convinced me *instantly*. This is very She. No doubts left. I kick myself for having so many years said to myself "I MUST go round to Bodley to see if there is more in Simon Forman than Chambers says." I have always put the thought aside by telling myself I was "too busy". But really I was too idle. Anyhow you have not been so, and have reaped your tremendous reward!'

In fact Coghill was not too idle: he was a full-time professor, I was a full-time researcher, interested only in pursuing the subject. He would not have been enough of a specialist researcher to deal with Forman's manuscripts; instead he did more useful work in modernising Chaucer's *Canterbury Tales* for our benefit – not many can read them in their original fourteenth-century English. Coghill had the indispensable gift of intuition: Chambers, a prodigious amasser of facts – had *none*. Hence he was wrong, not only about

Mr W.H., but in other books about Arthur of Britain and Sir Thomas Malory.

One Oxford man – in addition to close friends like Douglas Jay, Professor Jack Simmons, Wyndham Ketton-Cremer, David Treffry, Elizabeth Jenkins, Rosalie Glyn Grylls – saw the bearing of my discovery and was at once convinced by it. This was Roger Prior, of the Queen's University, Belfast: an Eng. Lit. scholar, but he was (and is) an experienced researcher himself. He knows more about Emilia's family, the Bassanos, or Bassani, than anyone; it was he who discovered that Emilia, Mrs Lanier, was a poet, from the incomplete copy of her poems, *Salve Deus Rex Judaeorum*, rarest of books, again in the Bodleian. John Buxton, an Oxford friend and a good scholar, knew this book but, unwilling to keep an open mind to any of my discoveries, he altogether missed its significance.

The trouble was not only that academic minds were closed but that *they did not want to know*. That is shocking to an historian, whose business it is to search and find out the truth and reveal the facts. But this is to fall down on their duty towards knowledge: it is the business of intellectuals to know, if they are to teach, and, if they do not know, to learn. *They did not want to learn*, and they resented being told.

Not so with an expert researcher like Roger Prior; he wrote to me, *à propos* of the Dark Lady, that it was 'wonderful to have spotted it.' Actually, thrilling as it was to know at last, it was not difficult to identify Emilia – the musical young lady notorious in the Southampton-Shakespeare circle as the former mistress of the Patron of Shakespeare's Company: it was obvious enough. I had far more difficulty in identifying Simon Forman's mistress, Avis Allen. For one thing, Allen – unlike Bassano and Lanier – was such a common name: scores, if not hundreds, of them in Elizabethan London. My research assistant and I searched through all the parish registers of London without avail. It was of some help that she had a rare Christian name, Avis. Since she was not in any of the church registers it occurred to me that she might have been a Catholic. Sure enough, there she was among the Recusant Rolls: a Catholic, who did not attend church. There were others, too, more difficult to identify than Shakespeare's Dark Lady – but of less interest to scholarship and the wider world.

Roger Prior is kind enough to write to me as 'the onlie begetter'

– that notorious phrase of the flowery Thorp, which has misled so many people into thinking that his Mr W.H. was the inspiration of the Sonnets. Remember, always, that Southampton, the young patron was the inspirer – not the only one, for there was the Dark Lady too. Mr W.H. was merely the person in that circle who had *got* the manuscript for Thorp. Eventually then there were two inspirers of the Sonnets, while the word 'beget' appears in *Hamlet* in the sense of 'get'.

People in the United States were more open-minded and generous, though by no means all. Professor Robert Kirsch, of the University of California, was enthusiastic about the discovery, in the *Los Angeles Times*. He took the trouble to come to Oxford and look up the references in the Forman papers in the Bodleian with me. He commented, 'I wonder how many more centuries might elapse before the right combination of scholarship and intuition would have discovered who the Dark Lady was – how much longer she would have had to wait.' That was perceptive of him, for – since I had not been looking for her — I had the feeling that she had been lying in wait for me. And she has succeeded in giving me almost as much trouble as she gave both William Shakespeare and Simon Forman.

Oddly enough, one of the most weighty, even elephantine, of academic Shakespeareans was in agreement with the early stages of my work. This was Professor T.W. Baldwin, of the University of Illinois. He was immensely learned, and would have made more impact on the subject, if only he had known how to write. But in the American manner he thought that bigger was better, and wrote immensely long books, so long as to be unreadable. One enormous book in two volumes was on *William Shakespeare's Small Latin and Less Greek*, with a sequel on *William Shakespeare's Petty School*. He was an exhaustive (and exhausting) authority on Elizabethan grammar-school education. He built up at the University of Illinois the finest collection of Elizabethan school text-books outside the British Library.

Thrilled as I was at the Dark Lady lying in wait just where she would have been – and a brilliant feather in the cap for the Bodleian Library and for Oxford – I was less excited than I might have been, for a life-long researcher is used to the unexpected turning up in documents. I remember being cold with excitement when, quite young, I made my first discovery in the Public Record Office. There turned up a pardon to Richard Grenville, when under-age, for killing a man one November day in an affray in the Strand, and then absconding.[1] He was fighting alongside a Devonshire cousin, a Speccot, of the family that succeeded to George Grenville's house of Penheale, and built the lovely Caroline stables there. What excited the then inexperienced researcher was to think that no one had known of this episode in the life of Sir Richard Grenville since his time – and how like him it proved to be.

As for the last fight of the *Revenge* in the Azores, the only account we had of it was at second-hand from Sir Walter Ralegh (as he always spelled himself – so I adhere to it, though rather inconveniently for USA). It occurred to me that there must be a first-hand Spanish account of the battle of Flores, and then found from Fernandez Duro's *La Armada Invencible* that there was. I was just in time, before the Spanish Civil War, to get transcripts of the documents from the Museo Geographico in Madrid. The excellent naval historian, J. A. Williamson, a good sailing man, helped me to interpret the currents, winds, etc. The result was that, in putting the two accounts together, Spanish and English, we gained a proper account of the battle, and of that Azores campaign, for the first time – one which overthrew previous accounts.

It was by a stroke of luck that I learned from my friend, Canon Shirley of Canterbury, that in the Chapter Library there lay the Diary of Ralegh's brother-in-law, Sir Arthur Throckmorton, which had never been studied. It covered just the years with which I was most familiar, from the 1580s to the early years of James I's reign – the years of Shakespeare's activity as writer and dramatist. A good many people in the Diary were already fairly well known. Again it was the unexpected that turned up: the revelation of Ralegh's secret marriage to Throckmorton's sister, Elizabeth, which earned their disgrace with the Queen, the birth of a son unknown to history, the *accouchement* attended by Ralegh's step-brother, the scientist Adrian Gilbert, etc.

There are disappointments in research, as well as lucky finds, awaiting the researcher. This Throckmorton was friendly with Essex, knighted by him at Cadiz, while Ralegh belonged to the party opposed to Essex and Southampton, Shakespeare's ambiance. A drawback was that so much of the Diary was concerned with Northampton

[1] cf. my *Sir Richard Grenville of the 'Revenge'*, 54–5.

– Throckmorton built a fine Elizabethan house near Towcester, at Paulerspury, where only humps in the grass remain and his tomb in the church. If the Diary had been more concerned with the West Country I should have been already familiar with some of the persons in it. As it was, I had to get to know Northamptonshire, places, houses, people, churches and who were buried in them – Elizabethans of course. Here I was helped by the denizens of the country houses, *châtelaines*, especially the scholarly Lady Hesketh of Easton Neston, who took me round everywhere. As an historian, from early Grenville days in the West Country, I took a hint from Macaulay and wrote down the places these vanished people knew as I had them under my eye. This helped to bring them alive.

When the book came out I naturally thanked these Northamptonshire folk who had been so hospitable and helpful. Some of them were grandees. This annoyed a provincial university professor – to whom I had been nothing but helpful, backed him for his doctorate etc. He thought that expressing thanks for the help I had received was 'more befitting a sycophantic eighteenth-century clergyman.' This, Readers – since I am writing this book for you, not for them – is what some creatures of academe are like, unimaginative and mean.

That book, *Ralegh and the Throckmortons*, has a great deal of original research and new information in it: about noteworthy people in the age, their way of life, household and building expenditure, wages and prices, craftsmanship, books, reading (it unexpectedly has some new contributions to bibliography). The book has never taken the place it should, for the new material in it, apart from anything else. Academics were displeased by the public notice the new light on Ralegh won, and have done their best to ignore it. Once again it shows them falling down on their duty, to spread knowledge.[1]

Those who venture in depth into the past may properly expect rewards: those who do not venture do not know what they are missing. After a lifetime of research in the Elizabethan age, I am more

---

[1] Today the public is becoming aware of all too many in the profession who were given permanent tenure in the Silly Sixties, but who have little interest in their subject and make no contribution to it. Those were the years when the Robbins Report was in the ascendant. Since these people were given tenure – everything was made all too easy for them – a problem for responsible authorities today is how to get rid of them.

acclimatised to it than to the shiftless society of today. Various bits of new information keep turning up, which throw light on the literature of the past as well as on the people. In Sir John Harington's *Epigrams* – the author of *The Metamorphosis of Ajax* was a kindred spirit to Shakespeare's – it was clear to me that the leading characters, Paulus and Festus, were respectively Ralegh and Ben Jonson. Others may have spotted the former.

Some striking pieces of new evidence turned up in the marginalia of Richard Topcliffe's own copy of Pollini's *Historia Ecclesiastica della Rivoluzion d'Inghilterra*: about the Catholic exiles, and notably about Anne Boleyn, whose innocence I have at last been able to establish.[1] Long ago, in my early days, I first brought to light, from an obscure corner in the Public Record office, the Diary of William Carnsew, which gives one an authentic picture of the life of an Elizabethan country gentleman in Cornwall. So researchers should never be discouraged: one never knows what may turn up. Nor should it be at all surprising that it should have fallen to a lifelong researcher into Shakespeare's age and time to have made so many discoveries about his life and work, placed it upon the firm foundation of fact, instead of worthless conjecture.

It is high time that an end should be put to the mess that has been made of the life of the world's greatest writer and to the confusion made of his work. I marvelled from the first why the Shakespeare establishment had not the strategic sense to see that, in the leading historian of the age, they had their strongest ally. They preferred to carp and obstruct, and since *in no single case* can they answer my findings, they simply sulk and keep quiet. As Roger Prior writes to me, 'the barons of the Shakespeare establishment cannot admit that they were wrong.'

For want then of common sense about Shakespeare, both life and works, they are persecuted as I am by the attentions of the crackpots. Only in the past months a lady has written to ask whether I do not think that William Shakespeare must have been a woman; another wants to know whether Queen Elizabeth I was not a man. This is not very different from those who would like to think that Shakespeare's works were written by Francis Bacon or Christopher Mar-

---

[1] v. 'The Truth about Topcliffe', in *Court and Country: Studies in Tudor Social History*, and *Sutton Place and the Westons*.

lowe, by the Earl of Oxford or Queen Elizabeth under an assumed name. It is all a frightful bore. The consoling thing is that the truth about human beings, if you can discover it, is vastly more interesting than the conjectures of ordinary intelligences about them.

2
Shakespeare's Autobiography

When I got down to work at Shakespeare's biography I considered what I could contribute that was worthwhile in this too much-trampled field. First, as an Elizabethan historian I should have an advantage in depicting the age in which he lived, the background to his life and work. Secondly, I had always been interested in local and topographical history; so there would be more to contribute in bringing the Warwickshire and Stratford background alive. Even the critics who could not understand, or digest, what was new in the book appreciated that part of it. Lastly, an historian's familiarity with politics would be able to bring out Shakespeare's exceptional understanding of politics and society. No-one had written about that – literary folk, even the best, failed in that field. Here would be something new and worthwhile; to my mind, this is still the part of the book that makes the weightiest contribution to our understanding of Shakespeare.

At the same time I took a big risk. I did not know that the 'problems' of the Sonnets, of the poet's autobiography, would all (save the identity of his dark mistress) work out in straightforward fashion. I had accepted the work of the usual authorities – who proved to have 'made such a mess of it', as Harold Macmillan said. They had never seen the significance of the obvious fact that Mr W.H. was the publisher's man, not Shakespeare's. Neither had I, until I got down to it: it proved the stone that loosened the avalanche on my offending head.

When we were young at Oxford David Cecil and I – both ardent devotees of the Sonnets – used to wonder who Mr W.H. could possibly be. We were under the misapprehension, like everybody else, that he was Shakespeare's young man. It was clear, as it had been to most authorities from Malone onwards, that the Sonnets were written to and for the patron, Southampton. But his initials as Henry Wriothesley were H.W., not W.H. And of course it could never have been William Herbert, for he was only a boy of twelve at the time, his involvement with Mary Fitton coming years later. Like everybody else, we thought the problem insoluble.

Oddly enough, it had not occurred to us, even to Lord David – who should have known – that no Lord could ever have been referred to as 'Mr'. It was not until some years later, with a fuller knowledge of Elizabethan society and social usage, that I realised that it was quite regular to refer to a knight as Mr. Sir Francis Bacon is referred to in the documents as Mr Bacon; so were others. Southampton's mother's second husband was Sir Thomas Heneage: she always refers to him in her letters as Mr Heneage – shorter, respectful, less pompous. But it is only in recent years that I have learned, from the standard History of the Elizabethan House of Commons, that it was the *rule* there to refer to a knight as Mr ———, followed by his name. So Mr W.H. could be a knight. People may be forgiven for not knowing that – Shakespeare authorities did not, Chambers, Dover Wilson, Quiller-Couch and the rest of them – so they were all at sea. Now that we do know that, we can draw the correct conclusions.

One further advantage that an Elizabethan historian had proved fundamental, i.e. in regard to dating. For want of a knowledge of dating and chronology editions of and commentaries on the Sonnets were all over the place, editors and commentators in hopeless confusion. Some literary editors – not Chambers or Dover Wilson – had seen that the Sonnets belonged with the early plays, as they do – but they could not prove it, make it firm.

When I got down to them I found to my surprise that the Sonnets were in intelligible chronological order: the topical references to what was going on at the time – which an Elizabethan historian could read, others not – consecutively 1592, 1593, 1594. This was encouraging, and gave one confidence; it was conservative and traditional, in keeping with the common sense of the matter all along. Moreover, the more perceptive among the purely literary had seen that the Sonnets cohered in language with *Venus and Adonis* of 1593, and *The Rape of Lucrece* of 1594 – which is indeed the case.

The Sonnets, then, proved to be in an intelligible order. No non-sense about re-arranging, dis-arranging, mis-arranging them as various people, with no call to do so, had tried, confusing people's all-too-confusible minds (A. E. Housman used to add, naughtily, 'if that is the word for it').

There is a complication here, which does hold people up, though it is simple enough and ought not to confuse any average intelligence. It is just that the Sonnets fall into two sections. The first section, Sonnets 1 to 126, may be called the Southampton Sequence, for the subject is essentially that of the poet's relations with his patron. The second section is concerned mainly with the poet's infatuation with the young woman, from their point of view. In date these come within the first sequence, and relate to 1592–3, for the affair with the Dark Lady is referred to, more briefly, within the first sequence. However, there is no point in trying to insert the Dark Lady Sequence there, for they too are in intelligible order where they are. It would be impossible. So, keep this in your mind when you read them – as you should, *as a whole*, like a novel or a play, for they make a most remarkable story.

Much of the incomprehension has arisen from reaching down a sonnet here, or another there, and thinking to get the hang of the matter thus. Of course an individual poem is to be appreciated as such in this way, but the complicated *story* of the Sonnets – they would make a play – not so.

Perhaps I have under-estimated the difficulty ordinary people, especially professors, have in understanding what is psychologically a subtle story, as one should expect with a mind and nature such as William Shakespeare's. Paradoxically, it should be easier for a modern mind to understand the psychological situation. No single Victorian mind understood it: they were mis-led by the flowery love-language addressed to a young man, even when they dared to realise that it was to a young *man* that it was addressed. This embarrassed them – just look at the embarrassment it caused Sir Sidney Lee, Professor Dowden and many editors of the Sonnets. I give some comic examples of their fumbling in my edition of the Sonnets with renderings in modern prose to help the reader.[1] A very able colleague at All Souls, Sir Penderel Moon, told me that he had never grasped their meaning hitherto.

Those who realised that the poems were addressed to a young man were apt to think that they were homosexual – notably Oscar Wilde and Samuel Butler, who had a vested interest in thinking so. William Shakespeare specifically contradicts this: addressing the youth he says:

> And for a woman wert thou first created,
> Till Nature, as she wrought thee, fell a-doting,
> And by addition me of thee defeated
> By adding one thing to my purpose nothing.
> But since she *pricked* thee out for women's pleasure,
> Mine be thy love, and thy love's use their treasure.

That is to say – one couldn't be more specific – the young man has a prick, in which the poet is not in the least interested. Everything shows that William Shakespeare was a strongly sexed heterosexual – not the slightest interest in homosexuality in all his work (a very different matter from Christopher Marlowe – or, on that point, from either Francis Bacon or the Earl of Oxford).

Shakespeare describes the feminine appearance of the handsome youth, with his long hair, perfectly clearly:

> A woman's face with Nature's own hand painted . . .
> A woman's gentle heart . . .

If only the youth were a woman! . . . A great deal is known about Southampton[2] at this time, and even up until after he was belatedly married, he was ambivalent, then bisexual. For long he refused to marry, though it was his duty to carry on the family, the noble house of which he was the orphaned heir:

> Seeking that beauteous roof to ruinate
> Which to repair should be thy chief desire.

The Sonnets began with the young earl's poet attempting to persuade him into marriage. Southampton had no intention of being roped and tied – even years later, in 1598, when he had by mischance

---

[1] *Shakespeare's Sonnets. A Modern Edition, with Prose Versions, Introduction and Notes.*
[2] v. my *Shakespeare's Southampton, Patron of Virginia.*

got Elizabeth Vernon with child, her cousin Essex – Southampton's adored leader – had to make him marry her.

In this situation the poet, who felt his responsibility in the matter, a decade older and far more in experience, did not want the young man's first intercourse with women to be with his own promiscuous mistress. This gave Shakespeare reason to worry, not only on his own account, but on the young man's. He felt doubly responsible – everything shows him to have been a deeply responsible man (unlike Marlowe, or Oxford). He was much the youth's senior, with a rather tutorial feeling towards him, and he had been responsible for the two young people getting in touch. With promiscuity, there was the ever-present risk of disease:

> I guess one angel in another's hell . . .
> Till my bad angel fire my good one out.

Informed persons know the esoteric meaning of 'hell' and 'fire'. But no wonder Victorian and Victorian-minded professors did not understand the situation or what was being said.

That is no reason why modern minds should be so imperceptive. An American professor, acknowledged leader of the 'New Criticism', Cleanth Brooks, laid down that Shakespeare's feeling for the young man was that of 'infatuation', for the lady in question mere friendship. How imperceptive can professors be? The exact opposite is the truth. Shakespeare was infatuated with the woman – he describes himself as driven 'frantic-mad' by her; his feeling for the youth may be described as platonic love – he was not interested in him sexually, as Marlowe would have been.

Here, above all, one needs to be immersed in the Elizabethan age, its language and usages, and to be able to catch the tone of the language. This *is* a subtle matter, for the language is certainly flowery, as is Thorp's dedication. But this was correct decorum for a poet addressing a young lord; when Elizabethans addressed the Queen they addressed her as a semi-deity, a goddess, Cynthia, chaste goddess of the moon, the terrestrial Moon, etc. Two of my closest friends at Oxford – even at All Souls – have always wanted to think the Sonnets at least homo-erotic, and would not take telling from me. This failure on their part came from their not being acclimatised to Elizabethan language and usage: they were thinking of it in modern terms. With their Public School background they *wanted* to think

the Sonnets homo-erotic; myself, open-minded, I would not mind
if they were – but William Shakespeare makes it perfectly clear that
they are not.

It should be even more obvious that the Sonnets are patronage-
poems, written by an Elizabethan poet to his patron; yet hardly
anybody has glimpsed this simple fact and its crucial importance.
They do not know enough about Elizabethan society. Yet it is plain
enough in the poet's public dedication of *The Rape of Lucrece* to
the patron: 'The love I dedicate to your lordship is without end . . .
what I have done is yours; what I have to do is yours: being part
in all I have, devoted yours.'

This is expressed too in the Sonnets:

> Lord of my love, to whom in vassalage
> Thy merit hath my duty strongly knit,
> To thee I send this written ambassage
> To witness duty . . .
> Duty so great . . .

'Love' and 'duty', those are the twin poles of the relationship, which
kept it constant during those years; in spite of the strains put upon
it by the incursion of the young woman and the appearance of a
rival poet for patronage, when Shakespeare's living (with a family
to support) depended upon it.

Nor would Shakespeare have stressed his 'love' for the young patron
in that public dedication, if it had been in the least homosexual.
Anybody should be able to see that.

Thus the psychological complexities and strains of the story *are*
difficult: the relationship of an older man, however much of a genius,
charming and witty, a family man, keen on women, at a loose end
in London, with a spoiled young aristocrat, also at a loose end in
another sense, well-educated and responsive, generous to a fault but
irresponsible. We have the growth from a protective feeling to a
kind of love; the strains of rivalry, uncertainty, recrimination, mutual
reproaches; yet always the underlying gratitude, for to it the poet
owed not only support, but greatest debt of all for a writer – inspiration.

We may now turn with confidence to the dating of the Sonnets. This
was not a difficult matter for an Elizabethan historian to work out

from the topical references, though no-one had worked them out before. Few though they are, they provide a consistent sequence, and thus give us a firm chronological foundation where there had been so much unnecessary confusion hitherto.

Quite early on, in Sonnet 25, we find:

> Great princes' favourites their fair leaves spread . . .
> And in themselves their pride lies burièd:
> For at a frown they in their glory die.
> The painful warrior famousèd for fight,
> After a thousand victories once foiled,
> Is from the book of honour razèd quite
> And all the rest forgot for which he toiled.

This is a clear reference to Ralegh's disgrace with the Queen, which was the sensation of the summer of 1592. It describes him and his characteristics clearly: his pride, his fame at the wars (France, Ireland, at sea); the fact that he was exceptionally hard working and painstaking (Elizabethan 'painful') – he could 'toil terribly', Robert Cecil wrote at the time; even his own language to Cecil, 'once amiss, all is lost.' We are in the summer of 1592.

Sonnet 86 comes at the end of a short sequence dealing with a rival poet, all in the present tense. Shakespeare has reason to fear his rivalry, for he is Shakespeare's superior. What is he rivalling Shakespeare for? – The patronage of the patron, i.e. the Sonnets are patronage poems in origin, written in the course of duty to the patron. That obvious point also has never been clearly appreciated.

The rival poet is recognisably described: 'the proud full sail of his great verse'; he is 'of tall building and of goodly pride' as against 'my saucy bark, inferior far to his'; his is 'a worthier pen', his 'precious phrase by all the Muses filed'; his verse is more 'polished', for he is a 'learned' poet (i.e. a university man). Moreover, he is aided by 'spirits to write above a mortal pitch', nightly inspired by a 'familiar ghost' who 'gulls him with intelligence' – which is how Mephistopheles tempted and cheated Dr Faustus.

Everyone would know to whom 'the proud full sail of his great verse' referred, for it was Marlowe's achievement to marry what Ben Jonson called his 'mighty line' to the drama. Suddenly, Sonnet 86 is all in the past tense: it is valedictory, something has happened to the rival poet; he has disappeared, and is not mentioned again. Christopher Marlowe was killed in the house at Deptford on 31

May, 1593. With Sonnet 86 we have moved on to the summer of 1593.

With Sonnet 107 we encounter what has been supposed to be the greatest conundrum of all and given rise to innumerable conjectures ranging all over the place with no sense of dating whatever.

> The mortal moon hath her eclipse endured,
> And the sad augurs mock their own presage;
> Incertainties now crown themselves assured,
> And peace proclaims olives of endless age.

Here Shakespeare, in his characteristic oblique way, refers to *two* topical events; two cross-references, corroborating each other, give one mathematical certainty: they must be happening at the same time. The 'mortal moon' always refers to the Queen: she has 'endured', i.e. come through an 'eclipse', a shadow upon her, a threat of danger. At the same time a peace has been proclaimed, uncertainties ended. In the summer of 1594 Paris surrendered to Henri IV, the long uncertainties of the religious wars in France ended, peace was assured. At the same time the Lopez conspiracy against the Queen's life was blown – whether he was guilty or not (the Queen thought not) – Dr Lopez, who had been her doctor, was a double-agent and was run to death by Essex in the summer of 1594. This made a great sensation; Shakespeare was close to the affair through his proximity to Southampton.

All sorts of nonsense have been written about those four lines, all of it, I am relieved to say, by non-historians. We will not waste time here by going into any of it – worthless; merely cite Professor Leslie Hotson, who ruined most of his research, as F.P.Wilson reccg-nised, by crazy conjectures. He argued that 'the mortal moon' was the Spanish Armada! Of 1588, years out: before Shakespeare even began authorship.

With Sonnets 124 and 125 we are at the end of the Southampton sequence – and of Shakespeare's sonneteering, so much the fashion in the early 1590s. We have his oblique references to the politics of the time – careful, prudent man: the blows of 'thrallèd discontent', the thought of 'policy', that 'heretic', while his devotion 'all alone stands hugely politic.' And, to conclude:

> To this I witness call the fools of time,
> Which die for goodness, who have lived for crime.

This is a plain reference to the persecution of the Jesuits, which rose to a peak in the winter of 1594–5. Their claim was that they were martyrs for religion only; but in fact their mentor, Robert Parsons, was a traitor, conspiring against the state, not only its religion, but 'aiding and comforting' its enemies, the Pope and Spain.[1] Southampton was a Catholic, but not a political one, hence never troubled on that account. William Shakespeare, an inveterate conformist, never one to stick his neck out (unlike Marlowe and Ben Jonson) expressed the point of view of government and people.

He takes leave of his patron in the next sonnet – thus the Sonnets ended that winter. What is of more importance is that it sums up, in most revealing fashion, the relationship between poet and patron. The patron's status as a noble is recognised, though the poet's love is not directed towards 'the child of state', nor was it anything to him that he 'bore the canopy', i.e. of a peer of the realm,

> With my extern the outward honouring ...
> No, let me be obsequious in thy heart.

In taking leave, the poet will still follow his friend and patron in his heart, and ends with a magnificent affirmation: he

> knows no art
> But mutual render, only me for thee.

We need not pause over this, for all that it shows that William Shakespeare knew his own value, for all the proper deference he shows to a young peer who was his patron, but also friend. Everything in both his life and his work shows him courteous and gentlemanly, able to hold his own in the best society, so far as he wished – and as little as he had time for.

Naturally there were *longueurs* in such a relationship, clearly and candidly stated:

> Being your slave, what should I do but tend
> Upon the hours and times of your desire?
> I have no precious time at all to spend
> Nor services to do, till you require.

This is Sonnet 57, mid-way on in his period of service: there we are in 1593, when he wrote the semi-autobiographical *Love's*

---

[1] For him v. 'Father Parsons the Jesuit', in my *Eminent Elizabethans*.

Labour's Lost, which makes fun of Southampton's well-known reluctance to commit himself to women. Then, in the next sonnet –

> Being your vassal, bound to stay your leisure.
> O let me suffer, being at your beck ...
>   bide each check
> Without accusing you of injury ...
> I am to wait, though waiting so be hell,
> Nor blame your pleasure, be it ill or well.

In fact he *did* come to blame the way the young peer took his pleasures: here was the tutorial side in the relationship of an older man to a younger left on his own, no father to guide him in the slippery paths of that world.[1]

It is all quite clear, though it is a subtle matter to catch the *tones* of the relationship, developing, changing, challenged, retrogressing, recriminating – as in all such complex intimate affairs; then reconciliation, *redintegratio amoris*, emancipation and taking leave. Perhaps, in addition to the contemporary Elizabethan perspective and inflexion, one needs to have gone through something like it to grasp it all. One certainly does not need it written about by imperceptive professors, with no such experience, intuition or understanding.

The dating – absolutely indispensable for a firm foundation and hence interpretation – is summed up for us in Shakespeare's candid, open way:

>   when first your eye I eyed ...
>   three winters' cold
> Have from the forests shook three summers' pride,
> Three beauteous springs to yellow autumn turned ...
> Three April perfumes in three hot Junes burned
> Since first I saw you fresh.

This is Sonnet 104, which would have been written in 1594. The whole Sequence reads intelligibly: the winters of 1591–2, 1592–3, 1593–4. Shakespeare first became acquainted with Southampton in 1591. That was the year of Essex's expedition to Normandy, when war was renewed in France and memories of war there under Henry V

---

[1] Not that Southampton's father would have been anything but a bad guide for him: his unsatisfactory career was a warning. He was stupid, obstinate and treated his charming wife badly. A political Catholic, he was twice in the Tower for his support of Mary Queen of Scots in the dangerous crisis of 1569–72. He ended up under the thumb of a man-servant, to the disgust of his wife, and died young, in 1581, aged 36. v. *Shakespeare's Southampton*, c. II.

and Henry VI revived. Southampton, enthusiastic to serve under Essex, got across-Channel, though under-age. The actor-dramatist first won popular success with the *Henry VI* plays responding to the mood of the time.

Here was something to draw the attention of the young peer, well-educated and interested in literature, to the playwright coming to the front. The poet wrote his prentice-piece, 'A Lover's Complaint', to win patronage, in regular manner, with its recognisable tributes to the youth's beauty and personality:

> Small show of man was yet upon his chin,
> His phoenix down began but to appear . . .
> His qualities were beauteous as his form,
> For maiden-tongued he was . . .
>
> That he did in the general bosom reign
> Of young, of old, and sexes both enchanted . . .
> So many have, that never touched his hand,
> Sweetly supposed them mistress of his heart . . .

There we have two of the themes to be developed in the Sonnets: the youth's ambivalence, his appeal to both sexes, his favours as yet withheld.

When the Sonnets were got hold of by Thorp for publication in 1609, 'A Lover's Complaint' turned up in the same *cache*, evidently belonging with them. Numbers of professors have doubted whether this early poem was Shakespeare's! I repeat Henry James's *cri-de-coeur*: 'Nobody ever understands *anything*.'

In my early work on Shakespeare at the Huntington Library, I had got as far as this, finding to my surprise that all was in intelligible order and worked out conservatively and consistently. All, that is to say, except for the identity of the Dark Lady, whom I never expected that we should discover. But there was no doubt about the young lord of the Sonnets – for all the foolish books written about the Earl of Pembroke and Mary Fitton; or all the nonsense putting forward various 'candidates' for the post of Rival Poet, some proposing Chapman, others Ralegh, one ass writing a book on behalf of Markham, the poet of farriery!

I was invited to speak about the progress of my work at a large meeting of the Modern Language Association of America, where the audience gave a welcoming reception to my findings. I followed Dr James McManaway, a permanent official of the Folger Shakespeare Library in Washington, their Shakespeare 'expert', a bibliographer. He muttered to me, beneath the applause: 'Still I shall always think that we shall never know who the young man of the Sonnets was or who was the Rival Poet'!

I did not take the old boy's reaction seriously – in my own mind I dismissed it. But in fact it was an omen. What it meant was that 'the problems of Shakespeare's Sonnets are insoluble, therefore no-one can solve them.' This was the orthodoxy of the Shakespeare 'establishment', and it was to hold the field for decades. So far from being grateful for having their problems solved for them, it annoyed them. They couldn't answer any of the solutions, or raise any consideration whatever to the later findings that followed upon them, so they closed ranks and erected a stone wall against accepting them.

An historian's attitude is completely different from this obscurantism. It is our business to find out, to research into a subject and to *know*. We welcome fresh light on a subject hitherto obscure, we are grateful to have historical problems solved. I had never met anything like this obscurantism before, and never expected the barriers that would be erected against the extension of knowledge about the leading author in the age on which I was an authority, in which I had spent most of my researching life and had already made several new discoveries.

In regard to Shakespeare it was the established scholars, the supposed 'experts' who didn't want to know or to learn. This was gradually brought home to me. A young Yale professor, at the university of Arizona, was a considerable authority on Elizabethan staging conditions. (I have held the tape for him while he measured Elizabethan screens in Oxford halls, typical background for the staging of plays.) He said to me: 'If you had come to them with cap in hand and said "I submit all this for your better judgment", they would have been better pleased.' I said, honestly enough: 'But I couldn't say that, for these are the answers, and they are right.' He summed up: 'Yes, they are right; but think what they would have done to you if they had been wrong!'

In fact, I would never have submitted my work for the 'better judgment' of such people. That would be contrary to the order of nature: it is for the third-rate to try and understand the findings of first-rate scholarship. That is the way in which knowledge is advanced: it is not for the first-rate to follow the opinions of the third-rate. In the proper process of the diffusion of knowledge, it is for the *second*-rate to dispense first-rate scholarship and explain it to ordinary people beyond rating. This is where they have fallen down, the most part of the Shakespeare establishment. I was only gradually to realise this as they built up their Chinese wall of incomprehension, then obtuse obstruction.

One objection raised to my findings was that Shakespeare, a mere actor, could not have been on those intimate terms with a young earl. There was an obvious answer to that. When Shakespeare's fellow actor, Richard Burbage, died in 1619 the Earl of Pembroke could not bear to go on from a reception for a French ambassador to see a play: 'which I, being tender-hearted, could not endure to see so soon after the loss of my old acquaintance Burbage.' If that is what one earl felt about Burbage there is nothing surprising about what another earl felt for his poet, altogether more of a gentleman than Burbage was.

Here is the place to point out to those who don't know the social etiquette of the age – as few do – that Shakespeare's being a gentleman, insisting on it and recognised as such ('Master Shakespeare' he was regularly referred to), is of importance socially. A gentleman could be on terms with an earl, a lower-class man would not be. This is still true in old-fashioned society, though in the social confusion of an egalitarian world, people may not know it. A servant addresses a duke as 'your Grace'; a gentleman writes to him as 'my dear Duke.' These things may not be important today, but they are necessary to understanding hierarchical Elizabethan society. They raise special difficulties for American professors, committedly democratic, like Professor Harbage of Harvard, who consequently got the whole business of 'Shakespeare's Audience' wrong.[1] Facts remain facts, and I have survived to rub them in.

In that year of the Quatercentenary of Shakespeare's birth, 1964, I was invited to speak at Stratford, where Professor Dover Wilson seconded the vote of thanks. After lunch I imparted to him that the

[1] See later p. 97.

problems of the Sonnets (except always for the Dark Lady) had solved themselves, worked out rationally and consistently. He asked, with eagerness, 'then who *is* the young man?' I replied: 'the obvious person, the patron, young Southampton.' At this he was visibly taken aback. I offered to send him my book with all the evidence set out. He objected that he couldn't read it, he was going blind. I said, 'but you can have it read to you.' He replied that, in his edition for the Cambridge Shakespeare, he was so far on the other line that he could not go back on it!

Now this, to an historian, was really shocking. Historians regard it as an absolute duty to revise their statements in accordance with the evidence. So too scientists. If a single fact comes to light which contradicts our statement, it must be corrected. The result is that Dover Wilson's edition is, like so much of his work, not wholly without value, but unreliable and erratic. Notwithstanding, he produced that very year a little book, *An Introduction to the Sonnets of Shakespeare for the Use of Historians and Others.*

This was meant for me, though I took no notice of it – irrelevant as it was from a non-historian in a muddle about dating. Like everybody else he had not noticed that Mr W. H. was the publisher's man, not Shakespeare's, committed himself to the misapprehension that he was the man in the Sonnets and concluded that they were addressed to Pembroke! When they began in 1592, urging the young man to marry and carry on the family, Lord Herbert as he was then, was aged twelve.[1] Really! All this comes partly from a non-historian's having no idea of *dating*: hence the necessity of an historian to help them out of the bog they get themselves into.

A bigger and more cautious scholar than Dover Wilson – E. K. Chambers – got into similar difficulties through not noticing the one obvious little fact and its significance. He too, in a vacuum, havered and hovered until 'on the whole I think that, if we are to look in the ranks of the higher nobility, it is Herbert rather than Southampton who affords the most plausible identification for Shakespeare's friend.' He then hesitates, 'but I have no candidate to propose.' He stumbles further into the mire. He thinks that 'the proud full sail of his great verse' 'ought to mean Spenser, or failing him, Daniel or perhaps Dray-

---

[1] And note, that by 1609, when the Sonnets were at length published, he had become Lord Pembroke. No Mr W. H. about it. Observe what a muddle all the Herbert-nonsense is.

ton. Marlowe's death in 1593 probably puts him out of question.' 'Plausible', 'probably', no 'candidate' – Chambers evidently was at sea. And we have seen that it is precisely that date 1593 that Sonnet 86 refers to, confirming Marlowe's death. That settled the identity of the Rival Poet for Professor Bakeless, then the leading authority on Marlowe.

Sir Edmund Chambers, a life-long authoritarian civil servant, piled up an enormous mountain of work on the Medieval Stage, on the Elizabethan Stage and its denizens, and on Shakespeare. We are indebted to his encyclopaedic research, which is invaluable, at its best in the documents. At the time I described him as 'massive but imperceptive.' He was not wholly imperceptive. He had a cautious suspicion that Mr W. H. might have been Sir William Harvey, Southampton's step-father, but did not see the consequences that followed from that.

What a muddle they were all in! Dover Wilson was a different case: almost youthfully eager and enthusiastic, he was often perceptive, but notoriously impetuous and rash.[1]

By deferring to these respected authorities it is no wonder that the public has been left in such confusion, the gate left unnecessarily open to the crackpots. One man, Calvin B. Hoffman, dedicated his whole life, and achieved widespread publicity by it, to propagating the fatuity that Marlowe wrote Shakespeare's plays. I found this reflected in my fan-mail when an American lady wrote to tell me that Marlowe didn't die at the time we know he did, but lived on to write Shakespeare's Plays, join the *Mayflower* with the Pilgrim Fathers and end up in America!

Her nonsense is hardly worse than that of the American Bar Association – in the realm of nonsense all are equal. This body held a Cross-Examination to decide on who had written Shakespeare's works for him, and came to the conclusion that it was the Earl of Oxford.[2] This irresponsible peer died in 1606, *after* which date a number of the most important plays were written. No matter: a young sprig of the Oxford family kept the nonsense going.

[1] cf. his colleague Quiller-Couch's judgment in my *Quiller-Couch: Portrait of Q.*
[2] cf. *Shakespeare's Cross-Examination*. Cuneo Press, Chicago, 1961.

Obviously he would like to think that his (rather crazy) ancestor wrote the plays. Just as Delia Bacon of Massachusetts wanted to think that a Bacon was the author, and started the Baconian racket, upon which a fool in Philadelphia spent a couple of million dollars in the nineteenth century, in the hope of settling it. Delia herself ended in a madhouse. It is no less appropriate that the originator of the Oxford-lunacy was an American Professor Luny.

It is worth remarking here that these fancies spring partly from snobbery: their fanciers think that only an earl or some such could have written the plays. This again shows no social sense: it is never the earls who write the books, but clever grammar school boys like Spenser, Marlowe, Ben Jonson, Milton, Wordsworth, Coleridge, Tennyson, Arnold – or William Shakespeare.

We do not need to waste time on crackpots, we should ask why is it that so many respectable authorities have gone astray and 'made such a mess of it.' The answer to this is simple: *it is just for want of straight historical method*. You cannot understand what is going on in the Sonnets by reaching down one here and one there. That is all that most people do – read individual poems, separately from the rest; in this way a lot of innocents do not know even whether the flowery expressions are directed to a woman or a man. They haven't a clue.

The proper method is the historical one of establishing the firm foundation of the dating, from the topical reference; then, on that firm basis, the 'problems' fall into place and receive their solution. Traditionally and conservatively, in keeping with all the rest of the evidence, both internal and external, of which there is plenty.

The eventual discovery of the Dark Lady – quite unlooked-for and unexpected – was a heaven-sent bonus for sticking to my guns in spite of all discouragement, obtuseness and obstruction.

I followed up *William Shakespeare: A Biography* next year with a modern edition of the Sonnets to make them intelligible to the reader. Oddly enough, this had never been done before. There have been innumerable editions of the Sonnets, not one of them making the story clear, for they had not the clue: no-one had worked out the proper interpretation of Thorp's dedication. I must admit that this is confusing and difficult, and to people with no knowledge of

Elizabethan usage, the personalities in question, *and* the dating –
a tall order – impossible to interpret. I had worked it out, following
the obvious clue everybody had overlooked, namely that 'Mr W. H.'
was Thorp's man, not Shakespeare's. Thus *all* previous editions of
the Sonnets had failed to make the story intelligible, making nonsense
of it and misleading the reader.

I repeat that it is not enough to reach down a single sonnet here
and there if one is to understand the whole. They are in a consistent
and intelligible order as they are, and again as always I am in accord
with tradition. They record the central experience of Shakespeare's
life autobiographically – what could be more important?

So I decided to construct an edition different from any before.
On the left-hand page I give each sonnet, in modern spelling and
punctuation; on the opposite page a version of it in prose. Beneath
this are a few essential notes, giving what one needs to know, not
cluttering up the page with a lot of unnecessary textual minutiae
to put the reader off.

This job was not as easy as might be thought. It stands to reason
that one needs to be very familiar with Elizabethan idiom and usage
to begin with – essential equipment. Beyond this it is not always
easy to catch the *tone* of an Elizabethan expression; and William
Shakespeare, subtle man, often has an indirect, oblique, suggestive
way of expressing himself. Some sonnets are simple and direct, others
are complex and baffling; sometimes in the complexities of the situation he did not wish to be too explicit. In verse one can say things
that one does not wish to be too outright about – I know that from
experience. It takes a poet as well as scholar and historian to get
Shakespeare right.

Some phrases and turns of thought gave me pause; but by sticking
at it I hammered them out. I felt confirmed when one of the cleverest
Fellows of All Souls, Penderel Moon – brought up in the strictest
school of Josephan logic – said that he had never understood the
Sonnets until he read them in my edition. If that was true for him,
how much more so for the less intelligent of the Eng. Lit. industry.

Again I have no reason to complain of the reception from the
public in general: that book has gone into several editions. It has
been entirely overlooked by the literary profession, who have most
to learn from it. Is it possible that one motive is the suspicion that
it makes their confusions unnecessary and themselves redundant?

So far as I am aware, the edition has never been adopted into use in any university or school syllabus – where it would be of maximum help – let alone made required reading. Never mind – to adapt the Latin phrase: eventually the truth will out.

I suppose too that it is hard for the conventional to understand someone who is both traditional and modernist, essentially conservative yet open-minded, ready to experiment. It did not occur to me that this piece of work would in time lead on to, provide apprenticeship for, the much bigger venture of modernising the Plays. My work on Shakespeare has had a strange momentum of its own, leading me on, revealing things that one never expected.

3
The Discovery of the Dark Lady

Why the obstruction? Why the evident hostility?

We must discriminate here, for not all were hostile or obstructive. Those who were most generous and welcoming were writers or actors themselves – at any rate, engaged in real work, rather than parasites on it. The novelist, C.P.Snow, who had also been an academic, wrote: 'a wonderful work. It shows what a first-class historian can do when he turns his hand to literature.' Agatha Christie, no mean Shakespearean and an expert in detection, saw that the problems (always excepting the Dark Lady) had been solved. So too André Maurois in France, attuned as he was to the English idiom, history and literature.

John Gielgud – never shall we see an actor more in tune with Shakespeare's inner spirit or with more feeling for the language – gave the book his blessing. Donald Wolfit, who re-created Marlowe's Tamburlaine on the stage, paid me the tribute of reciting a page of prose from my book, so he told me. It brought home to Harold Macmillan, an old Balliol scholar, 'what a mess' people had hitherto made of Shakespeare's life. Even among Oxford academics, from Christ Church J.I.M.Stewart welcomed a biography that was written by an historian who was also a poet.

The public response in America was characteristically generous, rather overwhelming to begin with. Invited to lecture at the Pierpont Morgan Library in New York the hall was packed, with an overflow audience in the basement. On my findings to that date a Fellow of

All Souls who was present – no Shakespearean but a well-known lawyer – commented laconically that it 'added up'. Myself, I knew that the findings so far were firm and unquestionable: I did not realise how much more was to come.

But soon sour notes were to be heard from England, in which the *Times Literary Supplement* gave the lead. We can hardly blame the editor at the time: we can appreciate the difficulties of editors, dependent on the 'experts' in their particular field. At that time their Shakespeare 'expert' was one John Crow. In accord with my regular principle we must say what we can on his behalf first. I believe that he was a good bibliographer, though he never got round to writing a book about that or anything else: he was just a reviewer of other people's work. It transpired that he had had an interesting, variegated life; he had been a waiter, handyman, pugilist. Anyway, he had material for a fascinating autobiography; he never wrote it. He had the sub-Chestertonian affectation of making his way in the United States by jokes at Americans. I do not find that funny, but then I never knew him. He lived somewhere in the suburbs of Oxford near the railway station; he never appeared at All Souls to my knowledge.

In a long, leading review *he* could condemn my biography as a 'fat, bad book'. No recognition of what was new in it, the way it reduced the so-called 'problems' that had puzzled people for generations to irrefutable common sense. No historian, he could not recognise the word 'Erasmian' as referring to Erasmus – just used it for a vulgar joke about soap. He thought it a mistake on my part for 'Erastian', a word he could recognise, evidently not knowing the distinction between Erasmus and Erastus, if indeed he knew who the latter was.

Enough about this fellow, now dead and forgotten, though not by me. His anonymous article, coming out in the *TLS*, with the authority it was assumed to have in those days, gave a lead to the reaction of the academics in Britain. Envious of the exceptional success the book had in the United States, they saw to it that the book was cold-shouldered in Britain.

My friend Peter Quennell – who won the scholarship in English literature at Balliol in the same year as I did at Christ Church – also wrote a Shakespeare biography. He had been given an advance to write it; otherwise – author of excellent books on the eighteenth and nineteenth centuries, his period – he had no special interest in the Elizabethan age. I did not read this book of his, but gathered that it advanced the conjecture that the Dark Lady was one Lucy Negro, an obscure black prostitute of the time! I expect that, today, Peter knows that to be nonsense.

But at an absurd event during a Brighton Arts Festival a year or two ago the demotic audience, carried away by sentiment for the black girl who took the part, voted that this must have been the Dark Lady. With my view of human inability to think straight I might have been disappointed if they had got it right. For, as the eminent historian Lecky wrote, people will decide against the evidence, or in spite of the evidence, but hardly ever in accordance with the evidence.

Hence it was to be expected that one bright reviewer considered that it was all right for Mr Quennell to write a biography of Shakespeare, but no call for Dr Rowse to do so. The exact opposite, of course, was the case. Peter's line of interest was the later centuries, mine the Elizabethan age, the proper background for a biographer of Shakespeare. I had long meant to tackle the life of the greatest writer in my period. But I had not told anyone of my intention, it caught them by surprise, and I think this annoyed them too. The success of the book in the USA did not give them any pleasure. Another *TLS* reviewer, following on, described the book merely as 'a triumph of promotion'. No recognition of what it contributed to the subject. Readers have no idea of what a motive envy is among academics, though it is obvious enough.

A more general motive, equally recognisable, was the Trade Union feeling: here was an outsider invading their field, an historian had no business in it – still more, solving their problems for them. This was a noticeable reaction, all too familiar in today's trade-unionised society. We all know the plumbers or electricians who will hold up work rather than allow somebody not in their union to get on with it. Here again my work and its reception have their sociological aspect, and the moral to be drawn.

In fact I did not belong exclusively to the historian's trade union: I have always been ambivalent between history and literature. It was the dons at Christ Church who pressed me into taking the History School. I should be more grateful to them than I was, for it was a far better School than Eng. Lit., regarded at Oxford as a soft option.

The History School was altogether stiffer and better training, most of all for research. I found it uphill going, but emerged at the end with one of the best Firsts of that year, followed by winning a prize Fellowship at All Souls, which I could never have done then from the School of Eng. Lit. So naturally we do not think very highly of seconds in Eng. Lit. – not a good class – of such literary experts as Professor Kenneth Muir or Professor Wilson Knight (who could not even see the obvious personality of the patron in the Sonnets), or a Humphrey Carpenter, biographer of Auden, whom he did not know. Wystan indeed was awarded a Third in that same school, and what he wrote about Shakespeare was erratic and unreliable.

From the pure historians' trade union I have been described as a 'literary historian', by a professor who was a Public Record Office man. In fact I spent years of research in the Record Office, and though rather claustrophobic I found it had an esoteric charm.

From the side of the literary trade union I found myself disconsidered as a mere historian. They have all along neglected, if not depreciated, my poetry to which I attach far more importance than to historical research: the poetry contains the inner life, the history books the outer. One can say anything in verse – people will not understand. From my schooldays I was writing poetry and having it published, many years before I dared to undertake a work of research. And have continued to write poetry all my life, when moved to do so – not on a professional basis. Professional poets all write too much: look at Wordsworth, Southey, Keats, or Tennyson, Browning, William Morris, Robert Bridges, Kipling, Hardy. A.E.Housman, my mentor, did not write too much.

In the over-specialisation that is rife today academic work is much too compartmented: historians are insufficiently literary and many do not know how to write; while Eng. Lit. people know no history and cannot even appreciate what they lose by it. I favour the cross-fertilisation of the two disciplines, sympathetic to both.

So far from this, in the last generation there was a ludicrous exclusion of the historical and biographical in the English Literature schools both at Oxford and at Cambridge. At Oxford C.S.Lewis dismissed any interest in the lives of writers, as throwing any light on their work, as the 'Personal Heresy'. It would, of course, be 'heresy' to this dogmatic Ulsterman, if he disapproved of it. At Cambridge, Leavis, Richards and Co. also dismissed history and biography: they thought it sufficient to concentrate on the text, the phrase, the word, without further enlightenment.

This is like the Silly Sartre who argued that, to understand a man, you need know nothing of his birth, rearing, antecedents or education: all you need is to take him as he is and analyse that. Clean contrary not only to all we know from psychology, but to common sense. This is the ass who thought that Stalin's Russia was 'the incarnation of human freedom'. How much more foolish can one be? It is indeed a question worth investigating why intellectuals are so silly.

Today another over-rated sacred cow, Samuel Beckett, informs us: 'The author is never interesting.' Is this true of Dickens or Balzac, Byron or Scott, Tolstoy, Dostoievsky, Milton or Shakespeare? The man is a fool to say such a thing, if he really thinks it. The technique is all too obvious: you draw attention to yourself by inverting common sense. Beckett got the idea from his fellow Irishman, Oscar Wilde.

Eliot gave his imprimatur to the depreciation of the personal and biographical, though what more acutely personal poetry than his could there be? And what a marvellous autobiography, bridging the Atlantic, he could have given us if he had chosen! Ironically, too, no one's personal life among modern writers is more eagerly sought for – perhaps that is why he kept it from view. (Wyndham Lewis to me: 'he's so *sly*.') Auden followed in the footsteps of the master: 'on principle I object to biographies of artists, since I do not believe the knowledge of their private lives sheds any significant light on their works'.

This was Eng. Lit. orthodoxy a generation ago. It was always silly, and in any event undiscriminating. For the light that *is* thrown on the work varies with the writer: it is at its maximum with egoistic writers like Milton and Byron, Voltaire or Tolstoy. We may readily agree that it is less important with un-egoistic writers like Fielding or Jane Austen, or even for Shakespeare; but it still is important.

This exclusion, or depreciation, of the personal and biographical, rests on a simple intellectual confusion. Of course the critical, aesthetic *judgment* of a work of art rests on those grounds, its artistic merit, its accordance with standards of criticism (though they vary considerably with time and circumstance). But that does not mean that the life of the artist throws no light on his work: it does not determine one's critical judgment, but it always helps understanding.

For years I had been working my way into Elizabethan society to form the subject of the final volume of my main work, *The Elizabethan Age: The Life of the Society*. It occurred to me that the papers and case-books of Simon Forman, medico and astrologer, would be a good source, across the road from All Souls in the Bodleian. I made two forays into these manuscripts, at an interval of a dozen or so years.

From the first attempt I retired discouraged. Not that the hand-writing was difficult, but I was put off by the astrological detail of the horoscopes, and also I had not then a walking *Who's Who* of the age in my head. Only Halliwell-Phillips had gone into these papers before me, an excellent Shakespearean scholar, best of them all among the Victorians. He had transcribed Forman's Autobiography for the Camden Society, which then refused to publish it on the ground of its sexual candour. That was no objection to me, rather just what I wanted: penetration into the crevices of the real life of the age.

Though Halliwell-Phillips was a good scholar, he made various mistakes in transcription, easy to do. Again I found that rather discouraging, and did not at first appreciate the fascination of Forman's autobiography or of his personality. A poor boy by origin, from Quidhampton near Salisbury, he did not fit into the conventional pattern. He was eager for knowledge, but frustrated all along the line. He longed to get to Oxford, but got there only in service to a local person, John Thornborough, who had patronage behind him and eventually made a successful career in the Church.[1] Poor Forman could not get entrance to a college – Magdalen – where he waited on his master, keen on sport and wenching, with evident resentment. Simon developed an understandable inferiority-complex, the makings of the sense of persecution from which he later suffered.

For he became an empiric, an unlicensed practitioner of medicine, constantly persecuted by the Royal College of Physicians, as all such were. To this day, in the *Dictionary of National Biography* and other

---

[1] For him v. 'Bishop Thornborough: a Clerical Careerist' in *For Veronica Wedgwood These*, ed. Richard Ollard and P. Tudor-Craig.

reference books, Forman is regularly described as a crank and a charlatan. This is incorrect. Of course Forman was odd man out – this
is what makes him so interesting. Anyone who knows the noxious
prescriptions of the licensed physicians of the age would probably
prefer to have been treated by Forman, as a great many were.

For one thing, he was less addicted to bleeding people than the
regular medicine men; in this he was right – even in the nineteenth
century the great Italian statesman, Cavour, was simply bled to death
by the doctors. For another thing, Forman did not think that urine
tests told one everything. He also favoured herbal treatment, some
of which might have been useful, others harmless. One dangerous
mineral he was apt to use, antimony, but this was in accord with
the Paracelsan medicine of the time, also disapproved by the College
of Physicians. They persecuted Surgeons too. Mercury was used fairly
generally for venereal disease – so rife in Elizabethan London – and
that also was dangerous.

On the whole Forman was a good thing, though not very respectable, and must certainly not be dismissed as a crank or a charlatan:
he was, in the exact use of the term, an empiric. He was certainly
an experimenter sexually with the women available to him. Who
are we to disapprove? All the more revealing of the life of the age
– that was just what I was looking for. If we are to understand
an age properly, to know its sex-life is essential. And, *à propos*,
William Shakespeare was the sexiest writer in the age. I have been
reproved for saying that also. I repeat it. The more you know of
Elizabethan language, puns, innuendos, bawdy, the more suggestive
Shakespeare becomes. It is a salty element that keeps his work alive,
a preservative. Victorian prigs, like Robert Bridges, could not bear
it; so his understanding of the plays was incomplete, his own plays
utterly dead.

What of Forman as astrologer?

Here again a knowledge of the age is necessary to get that right.
Everybody then believed to some extent in astrology, and the relevance of astrological forecasts. Since sun and moon had an obvious
influence upon this planet, then why not other planets? The influences
people believed in are reflected still in our language: mercurial, mar-
tial, saturnine, etc.

I was not interested in Forman's astrology as such; on the other
hand, one aspect of the horoscopes he drew for his clients was of

the highest value. It was essential for their purposes to get the exact date of birth – year, month, day, if possible hour: one can see the value that would have for our knowledge of the clients who came to him. They came from all classes of society, a spectrum from the highest to the lowest: from the family of Lord Chamberlain Hunsdon, first cousin of the Queen, to the wives of poor sailors from Rotherhithe or Wapping seeking information about the ships on which their men had sailed. So too many respected members of middle-class society, of City Companies like the Ironmongers or Grocers, who sought information about the prospects of their 'argosies' in the Mediterranean.

Forman had for many years known Lord Hunsdon's son and heir, Sir George Carey – who was to become the second Lord and follow his father as Lord Chamberlain, hence patron of Shakespeare's Company. His sister, Lady (Margaret) Hoby, a lady-in-waiting to the Queen, was a frequent client of Forman's for her arthritic complaint, and was able to inform him of her brother's ill-health. He suffered from venereal disease – his shaky handwriting betrays his palsy – and went to Bath for treatment, as people did. (It seems that Shakespeare went similarly to Bath, at the sudden breaking-off of the Dark Lady sonnets, with his dismissal by that promiscuous young woman.)

Forman was a keen playgoer, as he was a practical observer of everything human. Shakespeare scholars were familiar enough with Forman's report of three or four plays, seen at the Globe in 1611, but no-one thought of pursuing his associations with the Hunsdon family or saw its relevance. Yet anything to do with the patron of Shakespeare's Company was relevant and might turn up rewards for looking further. Chambers, who was not a man of imagination, looked no further; Dover Wilson was not that kind of researcher. It was fortunately left to me – and what luck I had!

We must adhere to Ben Jonson's characterisation of Shakespeare as open, honest and free. He tells us *everything* about his tantalising, temperamental young mistress, except her name. He tells us that she was exceptionally dark, black hair, black eyes and eyebrows, her eyes 'so suited': this was unfashionable at the time, and other people did not think her beautiful, though her looks made him 'groan' – the regular word then for sexual desire. The next thing we learn about her is that she was musical: there is a whole sonnet about that.

We learn that her temperament is haughty and tyrannical, and the poet is subjugated to her will, whatever others think of her. It was the regular thing at the time for one to engage a social superior to write on one's behalf to the woman to whom one was making one's suit. Shakespeare had called on his young patron for the purpose, and she had used the opportunity, naturally enough, to ensnare the un-engaged young peer:

> He learned but surety-like to write for me,
> Under that bond that him as fast doth bind.

This piece of information is followed by two bawdy sonnets to make one laugh. One laughs still more at the embarrassed ineptitude with which the professors have commented on them. They have not only Shakespeare's usual double-talk but also his *double-entendres*, so that perhaps one may forgive simple-minded professors for 'making a mess of it'. We can give them a clue by telling them that in Elizabethan language the word 'will' had sexual overtones, stood shortly for sex. One should hardly need to tell them that 'Will' also stood for William Shakespeare. So –

> Whoever hath her wish, thou hast thy will,
> And will to boot, and Will in overplus:
> More than enough am I that vex thee still
> To thy sweet will making addition thus.

We should know now what Will Shakespeare meant by 'addition', and what he was adding – from the earlier sonnet to the young man, in which he regretted that Nature had defeated him by 'adding one thing to my purpose nothing'.

And so this later sonnet goes naughtily on:

> Wilt thou, whose will is large and spacious,
> Not once vouchsafe to hide my will in thine?
> Shall will in others seem right gracious,
> And in my will no fair acceptance shine?

He goes on to urge that he might be one in her 'store's account', along with others: another 'scalp', to vary the image imprecisely.

> So thou, being rich in will, add to thy will
> One will of mine, to make thy large will more . . .
> And then thou lov'st me, for my name is Will.

The comments of the professors are even more comic than the sonnet. One of them interprets 'store's account' as 'the inventory of your property'. 'Receipt' is explained as 'capacity, power of receiving and containing (Schmidt)' – but receiving and containing what? The phrase 'of many mine being one / May stand in number' is thus interpreted by innocent Dean Beeching, of the boys' poem, 'Going downhill on a bicycle': 'the poet here makes the distinction with the opposite sense: he need not be counted, but must be reckoned with'. Yes, indeed.

It is always a pleasure to show up stupidity; but the next sonnet makes the situation all too clear: the young lady is promiscuous:

> Why should my heart think that a several plot
> Which my heart knows the wide world's common place?

We do not need here to go into the complexity of the triangular situation that resulted from the lady's enticing the young patron; we know that, ambivalent as he was, he was more capable of defending himself than a strongly sexed heterosexual would be. Here we are merely adding up the characteristics that Shakespeare allots the lady.

Others disapprove of her, in fact 'abhor' her: she is quite well known, and Shakespeare defends her against his own judgment:

> Who hateth thee that I do call my friend?

And 'what means the world' to disapprove his infatuation? The world is right, other people's judgment he cannot confute – but he simply cannot help himself. A well-enough known phenomenon where sex is concerned. The important conclusion for us is that she is well known to others to be a bad lot, in fact notorious: far from unknown.

However, her power over him is something abnormal: she must have been an exceptional personality to exert such an influence on such a man.

> O, from what power hast thou this powerful might . . .
> To make me give the lie to my true sight? . . .
> Whence hast thou this becoming of things ill
> That, in the very refuse of thy deeds,
> There is such strength and warrantise of skill
> That, in my mind, thy worst all best exceeds?
> Who taught thee how to make me love thee more,
> The more I hear and see just cause of hate?

We can only conclude from that: a very experienced woman. Also a social superior, for she looks down on him:

> O, though I love what others do abhor,
> With others thou shouldst not abhor my state.

Evidently she has been demeaning him with others. To that he has a just, if humiliating reproach:

> If thy unworthiness raised love in me,
> More worthy I to be beloved of thee.

Here is a revealing clue: she was down on her luck, herself unworthy. Shakespeare's love for her had begun out of pity: always a vulnerable condition for the man with a woman.

With his usual candour he sums up: one is no better than the other: both have broken their vows.

> In loving thee thou know'st I am forsworn,
> But thou art twice forsworn, to me love swearing;
> In act thy bed-vow broke, and new faith torn,
> In vowing new hate after new love bearing . . .

All commentators have taken this to mean that she was a married woman; but he goes on, characteristically, to accuse himself more bitterly – for all the time he was under her spell against his better judgment, against the evidence of his own eyes which told him what she was.

Evidently an unsatisfactory, unhappy relationship: she drove him 'frantic-mad', he says. In the end it was she who gave him his *congé*, or – as people would prefer to say today – the bird.

Several people, in the course of my delving into Forman's case-books, intrigued me greatly – none more so than the grandest of them, the stuck-up Frances Howard, grand-daughter of a duke of Norfolk, a client from early days. Daughter of a crazy Lord Howard of Bindon and dowerless, she had the sense to marry a rich elderly man, one Pranell (or Parnell). Left well-off, she was then equipped to marry an earl of Hertford, also elderly, and was left still better-off with her regular widow's thirds. She was now in a position to marry a duke and enter the royal family, with James I's cousin, the Stuart

Duke of Lennox. Not content with that she pressed him to acquire the English royal title of Richmond: she became known as the 'Double Duchess', buried magnificently in Westminster Abbey, as was Lord Chamberlain Hunsdon.

Another Frances Howard was also Countess of Hertford. A third was the wicked young Countess of Essex, who married James I's boy-friend Robert Carr, to become Countess of Somerset and have Sir Thomas Overbury poisoned in the Tower. She too was a client of Forman's, and her conduct bespattered his reputation: he had provided her with love-potions to compel Carr's emotions that way (he was heterosexual anyway, James I not). I mention these three Howard ladies to illustrate how indispensable it is to be able to distinguish one from the other in the Elizabethan labyrinth.

Shortly there turned up young Mrs Lanier, born Emilia Bassano, who had been the mistress of old Lord Chamberlain Hunsdon, patron of Shakespeare's Company, herself daughter of Baptista Bassano, one of the Queen's musicians. When pregnant by Lord Hunsdon, she had been married off, in the regular way with a dowry, to Alphonso Lanier, another of the royal musicians. This was enough to make anyone prick up more than their ears.

Evidently she was a person to pursue, and follow up her career. I found this no more difficult than following up the three Frances Howards, and far less so than discovering who Avis Allen was, Simon's own mistress. For Emilia came again and again. This was May 1597; her husband was at sea on the same Azores expedition upon which Southampton served. I was to find later that Lanier was quite well known to Southampton – since he knew the husband he might well indeed have known the wife. What Emilia wanted to know from Forman was whether Lanier would receive promotion, and whether she would become a lady of title.

For horoscopic purposes her information needed to be exact. She said that she had had hard fortune in her youth, her father having died when she was young. This was so, we learn externally, leaving her an orphan of six; from Bassano's will, he left a common-law wife who was English, Margaret Bassano alias Johnson, with £100 for the girl's dowry at twenty-one. Long before this she had been 'maintained in great pomp' by the Lord Chamberlain. He had apartments in Somerset House, of which he was Keeper; he also owned a house conveniently in Blackfriars. This was familiar ground to Shakespeare from his Stratford townsman, Richard Field's printing shop, where the early poems were printed, to his last days when he himself purchased part of the gatehouse there.

On 3 June Emilia came again to know whether her husband would obtain the suit he was after. Forman, with his wide experience of women, diagnosed: 'she is high-minded: she hath something in her mind she would have done for her. She hath £40 a year and was wealthy to him that married her, in money and jewels. She can hardly keep secret. She was very brave in youth. She hath many false conceptions.' It is difficult to catch the exact sense of the word 'brave' in that context: I think it means that she was well set up, for she had been brought up with the Countess of Kent, and said that she had 'been favoured much of her Majesty and of many noblemen, hath had great gifts and been made much of. A nobleman that is dead hath loved her well and kept her. But her husband hath dealt hardly with her, hath spent and consumed her goods. She is now very needy, in debt and it seems for lucre's sake will be a good fellow [we know what that means], for necessity doth compel. She hath a wart or mole in the pit of the throat or near it.' We may regard that as a beauty-spot, in the eighteenth-century manner.

Forman's encouraging forecast was, 'she shall be a lady or attain to some greater dignity. He [Lanier] shall speed well and be knighted hardly [he was not among those whom Essex knighted], but shall get little substance. The time shall come she shall rise two degrees, but hardly by this man ... And yet there shall some good fortune fall on her in short time.'

Here we should note the combination in this equivocal lady of high-mindedness, ambition, along with demeaning of her husband, whom she described dismissively to Forman as a mere 'minstrel'. Evidently she did not think him good enough for her, having been maintained 'in great pride' by the Lord Chamberlain. She had been married off to bear his child, a son called Henry after him – as Hunsdon had been called Henry after the King, who had had Mary Boleyn, Hunsdon's mother, for mistress. However, Hunsdon was not Henry VIII's son, but that of William Carey, a favoured Groom of the Chamber.

I have found nothing whatever against Alphonse Lanier: he seems to have been a decent fellow, whom Southampton befriended and got him a grant of the monopoly of weighing hay into Westminster, on the site of the present Haymarket. He was also a good friend of Bishop Bancroft, to become Archbishop of Canterbury, who loved music. Together they had served in the household of rich Lord Ellesmere. All that was against him was that he was not rich and successful enough to please Emilia. However, the son was trained up to become another Royal musician in that musical household.

Another side to her character comes out in her relations with Forman, who was all too ready to take the opportunity of her being 'a good fellow'. In September she sent her manservant to invite Forman to her house; she lived in fashionable Canon Row in Westminster. He 'went and supped with her, and stayed all night. She was familiar and friendly to him in all things, but only she would not halek.' This is Forman's regular code-word for sexual intercourse. 'Yet he felt all parts of her body willingly and kissed her often, yet she would not do in any wise.' This was provoking – evidently an experienced tease. 'Whereupon he took some displeasure, and so departed friends, but not intending to come at her again in haste.' She evidently knew how to keep the upper hand with inflammable menfolk.

Forman added a later note here : 'she was a whore and dealt evil with him after'. In this October, however, he was not disappointed : 'she sent both her man and maid: I went with them, and stayed all night'. At the end of the year he reminds himself to put the question what happens concerning her tales as to the invocation of spirits, whether or not an incuba, 'and whether I shall end it or no'. The last we hear of their relations is in January 1600, when Forman was at a loss to know 'why Mrs Lanier sent for me, what will follow, and whether she intendeth any more villainy'.

This adds further characteristics to our knowledge of this questionable lady: she knew about the invocation of spirits – one is reminded of

O, from what power hast thou this powerful might ?

She was evidently an exceptional, dominating personality – the only woman in Forman's extensive experience to have given him cause for alarm. She kept the upper hand throughout: his experience with her, also that of Shakespeare with the dark young lady.

It is essential to check on the dates, and if we can find the ages of these persons the story of their relations becomes all the more real and cogent.

In 1592–3, when Shakespeare's relations with his dark lady were at their height, he was 28–9. Once more we must see this in Elizabethan terms: for an Elizabethan – they grew up quicker and died earlier then – no longer young, in fact verging on middle age, in the sere and yellow leaf. Indeed his life was more than half over, for he died at fifty-two. Southampton, born 6 October 1573, was nearly ten years younger. That already tells a perceptive person much about their relations.

Emilia Bassano was born in 1569 – that much nearer to Southampton in age, four years older, but how much more experienced! On the other hand five years younger than Shakespeare. She had been married off to Lanier on 18 October 1592, fallen from her high estate as *maîtresse en titre* to the Lord Chamberlain. Five years later she told Forman that fortune had dealt hardly with her: it is clear that her experience of life was something exceptional and had hardened her. But it had not daunted her spirit.

I proceeded to follow up her career in public documents, mostly the State Papers Domestic: no difficult matter, for she turned out to be litigious, always sticking up for her rights. Needs must, for her husband died in 1613. In 1617 she took the lease of a house in St Giles in the Fields, to set up a select school there. This again was something out of the ordinary: I do not know of another Elizabethan lady setting up a school – she was evidently an educated woman.

It did not last long, there was a dispute about the rent – fortunately for us, for it yields us some information. She had been left in poor estate by the death of Captain Lanier, 'he having spent a great part of her estate in the service of the late Queen, in her wars of Ireland and other places' – to the tune of £4,000. Probably an exaggeration. But it is true that Lanier had served in Ireland, along with Southampton, in 1599 and we have seen that both served in the Azores Voyage of 1597. In an effort to persuade her to surrender her lease her landlord, a Morgan, offered to forego a quarter's rent: this 'she very scornfully refused, and said she would pay her rent as well as any

Morgan in England' – a characteristic touch. When she left it was without giving notice and without paying the quarter's rent.

Her son by the Lord Chamberlain became one of Charles I's musicians, but died in 1633. The 1630s are filled with her disputes and litigation with other Laniers regarding her late husband's hay monopoly in the City and in Westminster. She had made over her patent to his brother, Innocent, to enable him to obtain a new grant, allowing her half the profits. This was a source of continual litigation, petitions to the Privy Council and so on all through the decade.

We need not go into this in detail – it continued so long that at first I thought that it must refer to a second Emilia. But not so: it was one and the same woman, tough as old boots, who went on right into the Civil War, dying not until the spring of 1645, buried on the 3rd of April at Clerkenwell, aged then seventy-five or seventy-six.

This was not the end of her. I did not know then that she would prove herself a poet. It was not I but Roger Prior who brought to light her exceedingly rare volume, again in the Bodleian Library.[1] In 1611 she published this under the curious title, *Salve Deus Rex Judaeorum*. Why King of the Jews? She tells us in a postscript that she had dreamed this out of her subconscious, years before she thought of writing the poem – she was perhaps psychic. We must not go in detail into the poem: we are to look for her characteristics in it.

In this she shows herself next to the best woman-poet of the age, second to Mary, Countess of Pembroke. For an Elizabethan woman Emilia was highly educated, well read in the Bible and those classics to the fore in the Renaissance. This is already a contrast with many ladies of the Court, ladies-in-waiting to the Queen, some of whom could hardly write – Lady Ralegh's spelling was appalling, for example. The realisation of how superior her own talents were must have fed Emilia's resentment, another noticeable trait.

In versification she is closest to Daniel. She shows a natural aptitude for pentameter and rhyme, rather lax and long-winded – as no doubt in personal relations. Daniel was the poet of the patroness by whom

---

[1] v. my edition, *The Poems of Shakespeare's Dark Lady*.

she had been taken up earlier, Margaret, Countess of Cumberland, also unhappy in marriage, with a daughter to become famous, the Lady Anne Clifford, Countess of Dorset and subsequently of Pembroke and Montgomery. Samuel Daniel was brother-in-law to the half-Jewish John Florio, Southampton's Italian tutor, a member of his household and so acquainted with Southampton's poet. Here we should notice a tell-tale social difference. When Florio dedicated his Italian–English dictionary, *A World of Words*, to Southampton he does so obsequiously as a servant. Not so Shakespeare's dedications: 'No, let me be obsequious in thy heart ... only me for thee.' He writes as an independent gentleman.

On the title-page Emilia describes herself grandly as 'Mistris Æmilia Lanyer, Wife to Captain Alfonso Lanyer, Servant to the Kings Majestie.' Just as Shakespeare is always accorded the title of 'Master' as a gentleman, so Mistress Lanier is insisting on her status as a lady. She resented her ill-fortune, but she is as haughty and up-stage as ever. She garnished her work with dedicatory poems to James I's Queen, the Princess Elizabeth and Lady Arabella Stuart; those to the Countesses of Kent, Cumberland and Dorset whom she had known, others to Philip Sidney's sister, Countess of Pembroke, and those of Suffolk and Bedford whom she had not. The poem 'To the Lady Susan, Countess Dowager of Kent, and daughter to the Duchess of Suffolk', has some autobiographical references:

> Come you that were the Mistress of my youth,
> The noble guide of my ungoverned days ...
>
> And as your rare Perfections showed the glass
> Wherein I saw each wrinkle of a fault:
> You the Sun's virtue, I that fair green grass
> That flourished fresh by your clear virtues taught ...

This corroborates Forman's note, of years before, that she had been brought up by the Countess of Kent –

> Contemning Pride, pure Virtue to prefer,
> Not yielding to base Imbecility,
> Nor to those weak enticements of the world
> That have so many thousand souls ensnarled.

We may well doubt whether she had subdued Pride: her poems confirm her combination of haughtiness, consciousness of superiority, resentment, scorn for others. Her status was beneath what she considered her due; it was maddening to be so much more intelligent and to have got nowhere with it. But this was the lot of women, dependent on men for their status. This made her a feminist unexampled in that age.

She gives a hint of what she considered her due:

> And since no former gain hath made me write,
> Nor my desertless service could have won,
> Only your noble Virtues do incite
> My pen – they are the ground I write upon;
> Nor any future profit is expected:
> Then how can these poor lines go unrespected?

We see that the rhythm of pentameter came easily to her. The poem to the Countess of Pembroke recounts a dream she had had – here is the psychic bent once more. The dedication to the Dowager Countess of Cumberland is in prose: 'Right Honourable and Excellent Lady, I may say with St Peter, "Silver nor gold have I none, but such as I have that I give you"', and so on. That conveys a hint, in rich Renaissance prose, pearls of India, gold of India, aromatical gums, sweet incense, balsams, odours, etc. No doubt her tastes were beyond her means.

She had however enjoyed the friendship of Lady Cumberland; for another poem, 'The Description of Cookham', describes the amenities of visiting there where the Countess had a country place. This recounts the pleasures of the entirely feminine life there – for the Countess lived apart from her errant (and erring) husband, with their daughter: the ornaments of the house, walking together in the woods and hills, the favourite oak they visited, placing the Bible in a tree while they meditated or sang hymns. The Countess, being a Russell, was rather a Puritan – very unlike her husband. It was she who suggested to Emilia that she write a religious poem:

> Mistress of that place
> From whose desires did spring this work of Grace.

'The Description of Cookham' is a topographical piece, with a pleasant response to the beauty of the landscape around Cookham Dean: rather a rarity in Elizabethan literature, it is a wonder why nobody has noticed it.

It would seem that these delights belonged to some time before:

> And yet it grieves me that I cannot be
> Near unto her . . .

> Unconstant Fortune, thou art most to blame
> Who casts us down into so low a frame,
> Where our great friends we cannot daily see,
> So great a difference is there of degree.

This is Emilia's signature tune. Notice also her aptitude for alliteration, which comes naturally, if mysteriously, to a natural poet.

In former years she had happily taken part in the entertainments of Cookham:

> Remember beauteous Dorset's former sports –
> So far from being touched by ill reports –

this was young Lady Anne Clifford, later married unhappily to the extravagant Earl of Dorset –

> Wherein myself did always bear a part:
> Whereof deprived, I evermore must grieve,
> Hating blind Fortune, careless to relieve.

Nostalgically she recalled

> Those pleasures past, which will not turn again . . .
> Where many a learned book was read and scanned.

We derive a few more sidelights on Emilia from her poem to the Countess of Dorset. 'Titles of honour which the world bestows' belong properly only to the virtuous – though she had been anxious enough to achieve one in her unvirtuous days.

> Then how doth Gentry come to rise and fall?
> Or who is he that very rightly can
> Distinguish of his birth, or tell at all
> In what mean state his ancestors have been,
> Before someone of worth did honour win?

We need not wonder that her aggressive candour, sprung out of resentment and her experience, would hardly welcome her now in the company she had enjoyed in her attractive youth.

> This world is but a stage where all do play their parts . . .
> Here's no respect of persons, youth nor age.

She concludes with the desolation of the place when the ladies left it:

> This last farewell to Cookham here I give,
> When I am dead thy name in this may live.

Alas, it did not. Neither this poem nor the long religious poem to which it was appended, achieved any public notice or made the slightest reverberation at the time. Why not? – only half-a-dozen copies of the book survived: that offers a problem.

The book as a whole is dedicated 'To all virtuous Ladies in general', and there is a strain of aggressive feminism running throughout. After the first section dealing (oddly) with the Passion of Christ, the second is 'Eve's Apology in defence of Women', next, 'The Tears of the Daughters of Jerusalem', then 'The Salutation and Sorrow of the Virgin Mary.'

Mankind throughout the ages has blamed the Fall and Original Sin upon Mother Eve; women have accepted it, or had no say in the matter. Not so Emilia: she stands up squarely for her sex. Though smugly

> Let not us Women glory in Men's fall
> Who had power given to overrule us all.

All the same –

> But surely Adam can not be excused –
> Her fault though great, yet he was most to blame.

Adam had no right to lay the blame on Eve:

> That we, poor women, must endure it all:
> No subtle serpent's falsehood did betray him,
> If he would eat it, who had power to stay him?

Not Eve; her motive was to improve him in knowledge:

> Yet Men will boast of knowledge, which he took
> From Eve's fair hand.

Here is a reversal of the regular account of the matter which has obtained throughout the Christian era. John Milton would have been shocked, with his Puritan view of the inferiority of women. Emilia then extends the attack to charge Adam with responsibility for the Fall:

> he was the ground of all –
> If one of many worlds could lay a stain
> Upon our sex.

Thereupon she raises her banner:

> Then let us have our Liberty again,
> And challenge to yourselves no sovereignty . . .

> Your fault being greater, why should you disdain
> Our being equals, free from tyranny?

Raising the cry of Equality for Women – in the Jacobean age!
– I know no other instance in all the literature of the time. Not
until the nineteenth century do we hear that clarion call: today she
would qualify as a foremost voice for Women's Lib.

In the war between the sexes it is always men who seek to take
advantage of poor weak women – not that Emilia was weak, though
poor. Outward beauty, not stiffened by virtue, brought but dangers
and disgrace, as she well knew:

> Who glories most, where most the danger lies . . .
> For greatest perils do attend the fair
> When men do seek, attempt, plot and devise
> How they may overthrow the chastest Dame
> Whose beauty is the *white* whereat they aim –

the Dictionary tells us that this is the central part of a target.

In the sex war she makes only one concession – when like calls
to like, where there is sympathy:

> Spirits affect where they do sympathise . . .
> Beauty sometimes is pleased to feed her eyes
> With viewing beauty in another's face:
> Both good and bad in this point do agree
> That each desireth with his like to be.

Many women had been undone by their beauty – Helen of Troy
(though Shakespeare gave no good account of her in *Troilus and
Cressida*), and Lucrece:

> 'Twas beauty made chaste Lucrece lose her life
> For which proud Tarquin's fact was so abhorred.

She cites 'fair Rosamund', Henry II's mistress, whom Daniel had
written up in his *Complaints*, and Matilda, whom Drayton had celebrated. Emilia was as well read as she was talented. She did not,
however, want the approbation of 'the Vulgar's breath', nor of those
of mean degree:

> Mean minds will show of what mean moulds they be.

She was one of the elect few 'that wait on Poverty and Shame', and aligns herself with Pilate's 'most worthy wife', who was more worthy of respect than he was.

We are given a roll-call of famous women and their fighting deeds from ancient and Bible history. The Scythian women had put Darius to flight, even Alexander could not withstand them. She identifies with the Old Testament heroines, whose stories she celebrates: Deborah, Judith, Esther, Susanna. Naturally 'proud Holofernes' makes his appearance whom Judith 'had the power likewise to quell.'

Roger Prior gives us reason to think that the Bassanos were Jewish – as also were John Florio and Dr Lopez – and that Shakespeare was closer to the subject than people had realised in *The Merchant of Venice*. Emilia shows certain Jewish characteristics, perhaps not so much individually as in the combination of them. She was exceptional in intelligence and education, for the women of her time; this is not exclusively Jewish, nor are resentment, her abiding sense of grievance, her ambition and high-mindedness. But the combination of all these along with her identification with the heroines of the Old Testament would seem to corroborate her claim. And why should she have dreamed the title *Rex Judaeorum*? It had come up from her sub-consciousness.

In 1609 Shakespeare's Sonnets were published, by Thorp who had got the manuscript not from him but from, without doubt, Southampton's step-father, Sir William Harvey, who had succeeded to the goods and chattels of the house. The proofs were not carefully corrected, as were those of *Venus and Adonis* and *The Rape of Lucrece*; nor were they printed by Richard Field in Blackfriars. Nor is it likely that either Shakespeare or Southampton, now familiar public figures, would want their too intimate story publicised – quite a different matter from blameless individual sonnets being circulated among friends, as we know they were. Moreover, the Sonnets contained a speaking likeness of the woman in question, which we have seen corroborated by everything else we learn about her.

Immediately Emilia announced the publication of her *religious* poem, and in 1611 it appeared. Between it and the dedicatory poems she inserted a prose reply to her defamers. This feminist proclamation has a bitter personal note. 'Women deserve not to be blamed', they should not condemn each other, but leave that to 'evil-disposed men who – forgetting they were born of women, nourished of women, and that if it were not by the means of women they would be quite extinguished out of the world and a final end to them all – do like Vipers deface the wombs wherein they were bred.' This does not read like a statement of feminism in general: it is personal anger at having been defamed.

Why did her book make no impression, for all her care to commend it to the leading women of the time, some of whom she had known? Why, of this rarest of books, have only half-a-dozen survived? And why were not Shakespeare's Sonnets reprinted until many years later? After all he was the most popular dramatist of the time, the public only too anxious to scrabble for prints of his plays, good or bad. After his death his colleagues paid his memory the exceptional tribute of bringing together and publishing his plays, a big undertaking.

This is the only mystery that remains in regard to the Sonnets, about which there has been so much needless mystification. Here I agree for once with a conjecture, which we owe to an American publisher (not a professor): someone may have stepped in to prevent further publication. By 1611 Southampton was a Lord Lieutenant of his county, member of the Queen's Council, Knight of the Garter, on the Council of the Virginia Company on his way to becoming a Privy Councillor: he would hardly want so intimate a story made public. Would the gentleman of New Place wish to see himself in the humiliating light in which he appears in the Sonnets, both in regard to his patron and the dubious young woman who drove him 'frantic-mad'?

We know now what a very remarkable woman she was, a powerful personality. No doubt, when young and beautiful, musical, with a foreign flavour about her, and with that background, distinguished if equivocal, with her pride and spirit, she must have been ravishing, if not always ravishable. Hitherto people have made pointless conjectures as to who she could be, throwing any name up in the air, like throwing up a coin hoping it might fall into the right slot. This is no method at all; no wonder it yielded no results. I have said all along that the proper method is the historical one: first of all establish the dating – for which an historian is indispensable. Then patiently collect all the relevant facts, the circumstances, characteristics, ages of those involved, compare all the references, internal with external, for corroboration. If all these things corroborate each other and coincide, *with no single fact whatever against them*, then the historian – as a scientist would – has achieved certainty.

I have never had a 'candidate' – that second-rate cliché – for the position of Dark Lady. Wrong method! This is the woman, as Professor Coghill saw from the first.

When the news that the Dark Lady had come to light from lurking all those centuries in the Bodleian – just where she should be discovered – the reaction from academic Oxford was what might have been expected. With an historian's satisfaction at a problem solved and in adding something to knowledge, I assumed that they would be interested, if not grateful.

Not a bit of it. The reader should know what these people, in the academic world, are like. The professor who had succeeded Coghill was a friend of mine, Helen Gardner. She had been chagrined at Coghill's appointment instead of herself – no appreciation of the streak of genius in Nevill, of what placed him above the rank of the conventional academic. I did not know that she had taken the lead in trying to get C.S.Lewis, its most eminent member, off the Board of the Faculty because of his popular success as a writer. Three times I had tried to get her to support John Buxton's claim – a better scholar than she was – to be a Fellow of the British Academy. In vain: she did not think him up to it! With his knowledge of the classics and of Italian literature, which she did not have, he was ahead of her as a scholar, and wrote more scholarly books. I descried in her attitude not only a want of justice of mind, a common enough failing, but the familiar dog-in-the-manger attitude.

I was outside these amenities, not an active member of my own Faculty of Modern History, buried in research, which I much preferred to wasting my time on academic committees. Still, how much I missed the careful conscientiousness of the former head of the Eng. Lit. Faculty, F.P.Wilson! When the news of the Dark Lady's discovery came out, called on by the Press for her opinion, Miss Gardner immediately announced that there was nothing in it! Imagine this, dismissing it *without so much as troubling to go into the matter*! Without keeping an open mind even as to its possibility. And when the discovery came from a leading authority on the age, a lifelong researcher in it ... A sense of responsibility to the subject, our duty to advance knowledge, should have kept her straight.

I am all in favour of people having a good conceit of themselves

– La Rochefoucauld knew that conventional self-depreciation is only a way of recommending oneself. But conceit has to be justified by works, otherwise it is ludicrous. And Miss Gardner never got round to achieving a solid, substantial piece of work. When she sent me her little book on Religion and Poetry, she apologised for its being only a few lectures when she recognised that the subject demanded a big book.

Conceit and envy are regular features of campus life. It is like those minnows who could not see that G.M.Trevelyan was a great historian – accomplishing a big significant work, not once but a dozen times. To be fair, the minnows genuinely cannot see it. I once had to explain to a junior lecturer at some modest campus in the Middle West that Samuel Eliot Morison, like Trevelyan, was a great historian. He replied, 'you only mean that he is a great writer'! At that I told him flatly, 'if you weren't so third-rate you would see why Morison is a great historian'. Actually, 'third-rate' was too much of a compliment: such people rate no rating at all.

A well-known member of the Eng. Lit. Faculty at Oxford was J.I.M.Stewart of my old college, Christ Church. He had given a generous welcome to my earlier Shakespeare biography; so I asked him along with a few others to whom I imparted my findings in the Bodleian. This time he was obtuse, and announced that there were 'hundreds of whores in Elizabethan London'. This was most imperceptive, especially coming from someone who was also a detective story-writer. My readers can see – as he should be able to now – that Emilia was no street-walker. She had been the mistress of the Lord Chamberlain, a very different matter. One needs social perception in these matters.

At All Souls my friend Mack Smith, our prime authority on Italian history, said to me in no unkindly spirit: 'I couldn't care less who Shakespeare's Dark Lady was.' I replied: 'if you had discovered something new about Michelangelo, I should be the first person to be interested'.

Don't these people want to *know*?

At McGill University in Montreal, where I had given the Bailey Lectures after Arnold Toynbee some years before, my friend was the leading Canadian novelist, Hugh MacLennan, also professor in the Eng. Lit. department. A junior lecturer said to him *à propos* of my Shakespeare work, 'I don't read his books: you see he's not *in the field.*' What that shows is that the young man was not interested in his subject. Here again is the sociological aspect. Today in Britain there is widespread dissatisfaction with the universities: the public is beginning to learn that many inferior academics who were given permanent tenure without condition or requirement are so much dead wood.

A good historian always wants to know everything he can find out about his subject, and if one can only find out the truth about people it is almost always more interesting than conjectures about them. The true historian is not interested in conjectures, and we have seen in the course of this book that there is no need for them about Shakespeare.

With my original biography, I ventured to say that this would initiate a revolution in our knowledge of our greatest writer. I did not realise then that I was only half-way through, that there would be further discoveries about the plays, as well as that of the Dark Lady.

The attitude of the Shakespeare Trade Union in Britain soon made itself felt in the United States, where the academics followed suit and closed ranks. I had been asked by a friend, G.B.Evans, the textual scholar at the University of Illinois, subsequently at Harvard, to write the General Introduction to the *Riverside Shakespeare*, with contributions from various others 'in the field'. When the word got round that I was no longer subscribing to the confusions of the conventional professors, I was laid off from introducing the volume, and no notice of my work was taken by the contributors. Who remembers them now? My place was taken by an undistinguished professor content to remain in the rut. What a loss to the *Riverside Shakespeare*, which might have been first in the field!

Nor was I asked to lecture again at the Morgan Library, after the experience of those crowded audiences to hear 'the Liz Taylor of the Morgan Library', said Louis Auchincloss, the novelist. (I think I know who was responsible for barring any further enthusiasm.) The Folger Library in Washington was wholly dedicated to Shakespeare. There Louis B.Wright, a fair scholar in his limited field, and the conventional McManaway held sway. So it is no wonder that I was never asked to lecture there in twenty years – though the gates were open to Calvin B.Hoffman to hold forth about Marlowe having written Shakespeare's works. Not until Louis B.Wright and

McManaway had departed this life, and a new generation come to take their place, was I invited to lecture there as late as 1986. We may compare that with what the great Harvey had to contend with in his age and time.

The academics and 'experts' have fallen down doubly in their duty: (1) to get the subject right, now that it has been cleared up, rid of the age-long confusions shown to be unnecessary, reduced to common sense; (2) to alert the public, inform them of what has been discovered, and explain the new information, which will become traditional in time, once it is absorbed.

Since they have hardly yet begun to do their duty and perform their proper function – to disseminate new knowledge, not obstruct it – one can hardly blame popular writers, novelists, etc, for getting it wrong. Anthony Burgess, for example, missed a grand opportunity with his Shakespeare novel. I urged upon him the historian's conviction that the truth about people, if only one can discover it, is far more interesting than people's conjectures. Think what he had missed in not learning about Emilia, the Bassanos and Laniers (all of them musical like himself). He replied in friendly enough fashion referring to Emilia Bassano as a Sicilian! I should have thought that anybody with any sense of Italy would have known that Bassano is in Venetian territory, and that the Bassanos were notoriously Venetians.

Now too we can see that there was a double reason for Shakespeare's marked concern with Venice, a personal one in addition to the ordinary public interest. Of all Italy, Venice mattered most to Elizabethans: for them it was the Renaissance in full flourish. They could go there, when few of them could venture on to Rome (Venice was in conflict with the Papacy) – and scores, if not hundreds, of them made the pilgrimage.[1] A contemporary translation of a history of Venice enforces that 'Italy is the Face of Europe: Venice is the Eye of Italy.'[2] Over and above this general interest there is something personal in Shakespeare's concern, from the time of his entanglement with Emilia Bassano. Bassano and Verona were both in Venetian territory; *The Two Gentlemen of Verona* – I was first in all the years to discern, and prove, that it was autobiographical. *The Merchant of Venice* has this double fixation on Venice and the Jewish theme – and it seems clear that the Bassanos, like Florio,

[1] v. my *Ralegh and the Throckmortons*, c. V.
[2] W. Shute, translation of Fougasse, *General History of Venice*, 1612.

were Italian Jews. And what about *Othello*? We do not need to suppose that it was an earlier play revised; for it is clear that the factual range of Shakespeare's experience was not wide – neither the means nor the time for travel abroad. The *essential* experience of heart and imagination was concentrated in what he went through in those few years of inspiration and torment with Southampton and Emilia. And note that the theme of *Othello* is sexual jealousy. As also with the alien Cleopatra, his was a mind that reverberated, sometimes re-capitulated, experience.

Sainte-Beuve tells us that 'the men who make revolutions are always disregarded by those who profit from them'. Not even yet have they begun to profit from the revolution achieved in our knowledge of Shakespeare.

4

New Light on the Early Plays

It did not occur to me that there would be similar discoveries to be made in the Plays, awaiting one who was intimately acquainted with the life of the time. Even in the eighteenth century Dr Johnson realised that much more was to be found in Shakespeare if only we knew more of what was happening around him, not only topical references and what was agitating his mind, but what was the concern of the public. With what we should call today good 'box-office' sense the responsive actor-dramatist regularly appealed to this last, from the beginning to the end. The *Henry VI* plays owed their success to the re-awakening of war in Normandy in 1591; *The Tempest* responded to the public interest in the voyages to Virginia and was specifically sparked off by one of them.

Would you believe, that in our day most members of the Shakespeare Trade Union, though not all, disclaim any such knowledge, some of them so obscurantist as to deny its having any relevance. But every writer writes out of (a) his own experience, and (b) out of observation of what goes on around him; hence his knowledge of life, great or small, according to responsiveness and capacity to express it. Shakespeare was an acute observer of the human scene around him, nothing lost on him.

To excuse obscurantism, or perhaps simple inability to tackle the contemporary scene, the cliché ran that Shakespeare 'transmuted' all that, i.e. was not like other writers. These people do not know what real writers are like or how they work. This is simple 'bardolatry'

– what a Muggeridge, with his inexhaustible Christian charity, accused me of. The reader can now see for himself that my attitude was the exact opposite – reducing mystification to commonsense fact.

In any case I have never been taken in by the excessive claims for lit. crit. as an end in itself: literary criticism should set itself the more modest task of first *understanding* creative work in all its aspects, including the personal and biographical, and then *interpreting* it sympathetically and critically. It should subordinate itself to the claims of creative work, which are primary, criticism secondary. It is significant that in a creative age like the Elizabethan, with its immense productivity in literature and the drama, the amount of criticism is minimal. The best dramatic criticism of the age is contained in one scene of *Hamlet*. Today the upas-tree of criticism bids fair, or unfair, to eat creativeness up – everyone knows how plays on Broadway have to run the gauntlet of killer critics; Arthur Miller has told us how discouraging that is to dramatists. One might say the same with regard to poetry – besides the reversal of good standards everywhere. As Pope writes of such poets:

> And he whose fustian's so sublimely bad –
> It is not poetry, but prose run mad.

Remember, again, the emphasis I have placed on Shakespeare as the most autobiographical of the dramatists. I repeat it, since no-one has noticed it; he wrote his autobiography in the Sonnets. Other sonnet sequences were autobiographical in inspiration: notably Philip Sidney's, which describes his frustrated love for Penelope Devereux, Lady Rich – Astrophil for Stella and Philip – with its denunciation of poor Lord Rich for marrying her. Spenser's Sonnets are apparently devoted to his wife, though we know immeasurably less about her, in this poet's idealised strain, than in Shakespeare's uninhibited candour about himself and Emilia.

An important discovery in regard to the Plays was the latest in time, quite recent; but since the play is an early one we should deal with it here. This is the entirely autobiographical inspiration and character of *The Two Gentlemen of Verona*, which no one in all the centuries since had ever noticed before. Yet we should have done. For look closely at the subject: the rivalry of the two men for the love of one woman, Silvia. All commentators had regarded the ending as utterly improbable and unconvicing. One friend behaves badly and betrays the other; yet at the end the other hands over his girl to him on his repentance. With this inadequate excuse:

> Who by repentance is not satisfied
> Is nor of heaven nor earth – for these are pleased.
> And that my love may appear plain and free,
> All that was mine in Silvia I give thee.

All commentators have been affronted by this; but, in the confusion with which the Sonnets had hitherto been regarded, not one of them had noticed that this was precisely what had happened between the young patron and his poet. The latter, the faithful friend, had had to give way in the circumstances.

Yet not without reproach. Turn to the early sonnets that first speak of the breach in friendship:

> Nor can thy shame give physic to my grief –
> Though thou repent, yet I have still the loss:
> The offender's sorrow lends but weak relief
> To him that bears the strong offence's cross.

Shakespeare forgives his young friend, excuses him on the score of youth:

> No more be grieved at that which thou hast done:
> Roses have thorns and silver fountains mud;
> Clouds and eclipses stain both moon and sun,
> And loathsome canker lives in sweetest bud.

The breach is described in terms of landscape, the sun of friendship being clouded over:

> Why didst thou promise such a beauteous day . . .
> To let base clouds o'ertake me in my way.

Turn to the play and we find:

> O, how this spring of love resembleth
> The uncertain glory of an April day,
> Which now shows all the beauty of the sun,
> And by and by a cloud takes all away.

In the first scene we have similar language, the canker in the bud, etc, but also something more revealing:

> Yet writers say, as in the sweetest bud
> The eating canker dwells, so eating love
> Inhabits in the finest wits of all.

Who are the writers who say just that?

> And writers say, as the most forward bud
> Is eaten by the canker ere it blow,
> Even so by love the young and tender wit
> Is turned to folly, blasting in the bud,
> Losing his verdure even in the prime
> And all the fair effects of future hopes.

This is precisely the warning that Shakespeare has given the young man in the Sonnets, at having dealings with Emilia: he is the young and tender wit who may lose more than his freshness and the future hopes placed on his promise. But 'the finest wits of all' are no less prey to love and liable to the canker at the heart of it. 'Wit' in Elizabethan usage meant intelligence – we have not entirely lost that sense of the word though the modern sense is apt to be confined to clever turns of speech. William Shakespeare had both – and this is his opinion of himself: he knew his own quality, corroborated by what Robert Greene said of him at this very time.

His own experience at the moment is to be seen in –

> To be in love, where scorn is bought with groans,
> Coy looks with heart-sore sighs; one fading moment's mirth
> With twenty watchful, weary, tedious nights:
> If haply won, perhaps a hapless gain;
> If lost, why then a grievous labour won:
> However, but a folly bought with wit,
> Or else a wit by folly vanquishèd.

This was his experience with Emilia; we note his characteristic lack of illusions, the ability to see himself as in a mirror, a faculty doubled by his profession as an actor. We shall see this repeated too; for – another point no-one has noticed – his range of experience, intense in accordance with his nature, was comparatively small. He had to make the most of it: the rest was imagination, reading and reflection.

Now we know why no-one has found a source for *The Two Gentlemen*, as with nearly all other plays. The professors go on and on about its being based on the academic debate between the claims of friendship as against love. Somewhere Shakespeare says that friendship cannot be trusted when love breaks in. As we have seen in the Sonnets, love had to give way – precipitated by Emilia sacking him – to friendship; this is how it is in the play too, and why.

The play is as autobiographical as the Sonnets, its source the

author's own experience. Those years of the relationship with Southampton, its ups and downs, the competition for Emilia, the rivalry
with Marlowe, form the central story of his life. When they were
over, with the formation of the Lord Chamberlain's Company in
1594, with himself as a leading member, actor, producer, manager,
and its full-time dramatist, there was little else but his work for it
for the rest of his life. Too busy – that, and the rewards of such
constant labour to build up the position of an independent, propertied
gentleman at Stratford. That is his story.

Now, too, we know the date of the play, hitherto unknown,
with conjectures all over the place as usual. We have the firm dating
of the Sonnets, and the close parallel between the play and those
sonnets 32 to 35 which belong to 1592. The date of the play is
1592.

None of this was clear to me, or to anybody else, when I wrote
my original Biography. But I was already able to throw a great deal
of light on the next play, *Love's Labour's Lost*, which had for centuries
been regarded as a hopeless enigma with all its topical allusions,
puns, parodies, esoteric jokes. One theme was clear from the first
– the comic subject upon which the play turns: the reluctance of
the King (Navarre) to embark upon relations with women, and his
retirement with his courtiers into a course of study instead. This
was already a joke, for everybody in the know knew Henry of
Navarre's excessive addiction to women. The Navarre of the play
is, of course, Southampton, the theme that which I have called the
Southampton Theme.

Critics had already seen that Berowne 'represented', as they put
it, Shakespeare's own point of view, as against this: women's love
as the great educator, not books but life itself:

> They are the books, the arts, the academes,
> That show, contain, and nourish all the world.

All the same, the critics had never perceived that in Berowne Shakespeare was guying himself:

> a merrier man –
> Within the limit of becoming mirth –

a joke on himself and his fondness for bawdy –

> I never spent an hour's talk withal.
> His eye begets occasions for his wit,
> For every object that the one doth catch
> The other turns to a mirth-moving jest:
> Which his fair tongue, conceit's expositor,
> Delivers in such apt and gracious words
> That agèd ears play truant at his tales,
> And younger hearings are quite ravishèd,
> So sweet and voluble is his discourse.

One sees that, in laughing at himself, Shakespeare is not hard on himself, and it is revealing how he charmed the company that he was in. This dove-tails in with what John Aubrey heard about him: 'he was a handsome, well-shaped man, very good company, and of a very ready and pleasant smooth wit.'

Once one has the autobiographical clue one sees other characteristics he describes in himself: he does not subscribe to the rules laid down:

> As, not to see a woman in that term . . .
> And one day in a week to touch no food,
> And but one meal on every day beside . . .
> And then, to sleep but three hours in the night,
> And not to be seen to wink of all the day –
> When I was wont to think no harm all night,
> And make a dark night too of half the day.

You may interpret the innuendo there, in terms of what you now know of him from the Sonnets.

One leading character I blame myself for missing: the obvious identity of Don Adriano de Armado, who is the target for most of the jokes and exposures in the play. No Shakespeare 'expert' or Eng. Lit. scholar had perceived who he was; this was left to an historian, Martin Hume, who knew Spain.

> Our Court, you know, is haunted
> With a refinèd traveller of Spain:
> A man in all the world's new fashion planted,
> That hath a mint of phrases in his brain.
> One whom the music of his own vain tongue
> Doth ravish like enchanting harmony;
> A man of compliments, whom right and wrong
> Have chose as umpire of their mutiny . . .
> A man of fire-new words, fashion's own knight.

> But, I protest, I love to hear him lie,
> And I will use him for my minstrelsy.

The poet-dramatist of the Southampton circle proceeded to do so. This was the famous Antonio Pérez, Philip II's former secretary of state, who was now an exile, entertained on his first visit by Essex, Southampton's chief, at Essex House, where his personality became obnoxious to all. He was a professional rhetorician, who rated his accomplishment as such all too highly; he published his flowery Latin letters with their inflated compliments, he was a great flatterer, and a liar. As an exile, he wore out his welcome, was extravagant and a bore. Like his cronies at Essex House, Anthony and Francis Bacon, he was a well-known homosexual. So, in the play, he is made to fall – Pérez with his tastes, the refinèd traveller (he published his *peregrinatio*) – for an ignorant country lass.

Readers of this play will remember that the Princess of France, attended by her ladies, comes on a visit to Navarre-Southampton's Court. No-one had noticed that Henry of Navarre's sister, the Princess Catherine, had a similar Court of her own at Pau, and when she journeyed north to her brother, she had had Antonio Pérez in attendance. The names of the attendant lords in the play – Berowne (Biron), Longaville (Longueville), Dumaine (Mayenne) – are familiar to us from events in France at the time. Essex and Southampton were in touch with these and with Henry of Navarre; and the names occur also in the French pamphlets that Richard Field was issuing from Blackfriars at the time.

There is no mystery about Berowne-Shakespeare's lady in the play: everybody has recognised that she is the dark lady of the Sonnets, described in practically repetitive language. There we know

> my mistress' eyes are raven black,
> Her eyes so suited [i.e. black brows] and they mourners seem
> As such who, not born fair, no beauty lack . . .
> In the old age black was not counted fair,
> Or if it were, it bore not beauty's name . . .

Now in the play we read

> O, if in black my lady's brows be decked
> It mourns that painting and usurping hair
> Should ravish doters with a false aspect;
> And therefore is she born to make black fair:

> Her favour turns the fashion of the days . . .
> And therefore red . . .
> Paints itself black to imitate her brow.

More is made of her unfashionably dark colouring:

> Is ebony like her? O wood divine,
> A wife of such wood were felicity . . .

And so on. Such a talented young creature was a great contrast to a respectable *hausfrau* at Stratford; and leading a double life is more stimulating to the imagination.

The play also reflects something of what an older man had to put up with from a haughty and temperamental young mistress, when she says:

> How I would make him fawn, and beg, and seek,
> And wait the season, and observe the times,
> And spend his prodigal wits in bootless rhymes,
> And shape his service wholly to my hests . . .
> So planet-like would I o'er-sway his state,
> That he should be my fool, and I his fate.

'Prodigal wits', 'bootless rhymes', 'fawn and beg', 'observe the times', 'service' – how recognisable it all is, writing with his usual honest candour!

We need go no further into this play, always regarded as an 'enigma': we see that it is quite intelligible – though some of its esoteric language, its puns and word-play, require explaining. This play above all needs putting into contemporary language; to put it uncompromisingly – it *needs* modernising to be understood. A lot of the word-play relates to the schoolmaster, Holofernes. Remember, also, that the Italian-Jewish Florio was Southampton's tutor in Italian, who compiled an Italian-English Dictionary, *A World of Words*, with its definitions.

Hence fun is made of all this:

> The deer was, as you know, *sanguis*, in blood; ripe as a pomewater, who now hangeth like a jewel in the ear of *caelo*, the sky, the welkin, the heaven, and anon falleth like a crab on the face of *terra*, the soil, the land, the earth.

The curate says that the deer was 'a buck of the first head.' The schoolmaster contradicts this, in Latin, '*haud credo*'. Dull, the constable, misunderstands this:

'Twas not a haud credo, 'twas a pricket.

I first explained this Elizabethan pun many years ago, in the *Times Literary Supplement* in days more creditable for scholarship. William Shakespeare knew all about deer, he had also been a schoolmaster in early years. The buck was not of the first head, but a pricket, i.e. of the second year when its horns grow. Dull the constable mistakes the schoolmaster's 'haud credo' ('I hardly think so') for English 'aud grey doe' – with the English pronunciation of Latin in those days.

Once more there is no other 'source' than the autobiographical, Shakespeare's own experience in the Southampton circle. The excellent Sisson says 'the plot of *Love's Labour's Lost* appears to have been of Shakespeare's own devising'; then, being a professor, goes on to say that 'the matter of the play is the dramatization of the debate between Art or Learning, and Love.' An academic way of looking at it. If we knew more about the Southampton circle we should no doubt recognise more characters from it. In default of knowledge of the time, editions of this play have been even more at sea than usual, with ignorant conjectures of the boastful, loquacious Armado as Philip of Spain, the taciturn, secretive 'Prudent King'!

An even more ludicrous mess was made of the harmless reference to black as

The hue of dungeons and the school of night.

The phrase was erected into an edifice of nonsense by the fanciful and erratic Professor Frances Yates. She thought she saw a whole School, practically a college, of sombre writers, Ralegh, Chapman and others as belonging to it. All now recognised to be the nonsense it was all along, but not before another lady-professor, Miss Muriel Bradbrook, had slipped in the mud; or rather, as I was able to describe it, the 'mares' nest.'[1]

Everything relates the play firmly to the plague year 1593. In the last Act the plague is in the background. Berowne-Shakespeare says,

Write, 'Lord have mercy on us', on those three:
They are infected, in their hearts it lies;
They have the plague, and caught it of your eyes.

[1] Professor Bradbrook dedicated a whole book, *The School of Night* (Cambridge University Press), to this mares' nest. I hardly think it will be reprinted.

These lords are visited: you are not free,
For the Lord's 'tokens' on you do I see.

'Tokens' are plague-spots. The years 1592 and 1593 were years of severe plague, when theatre-playing was mostly stopped and companies dispersed about the country. These were the years when the actor was freer from acting, to write his long poems for his patron, the Sonnets for him, and two such private plays as *The Two Gentlemen* and *Love's Labour's Lost*.

In 1592 Robert Greene from his death-bed launched his envious attack on the successful actor turned dramatist, which has been commented on *ad nauseam*. Greene charged the actor with beautifying himself 'with our feathers', i.e. challenging the professionals like Greene at writing plays. He then identifies him by parodying a line from the too successful *Henry VI*; and 'being an absolute Johannes Factotum, is in his own conceit the only Shake-scene in a country.' That is, the new-comer can turn his hand to anything, and has a good conceit of himself. Both these characteristics we now know to be true, though it was left to me to point them out.

This passage has been quoted over and over again, but not what follows. Chambers, in his standard collection of documents relating to Shakespeare, omits it with his usual blinkeredness. He failed to see how revealing it is. Roberto, i.e. Greene, falls into conversation with a countryman, i.e. a provincial, who turns out to be a player – the profession which gets 'by scholars their whole living.' Here was proper trade-union feeling: he meant by 'scholars', university intellectuals like himself.

"A player!", quoth Roberto, "I took you rather for a *gentleman*, of great living, for ... by outward habit you would be taken for a substantial man." "So I am, where I dwell," quoth the player, "reputed able at my proper cost to build a windmill. What though the world once went hard with me, when I was fain to carry my playing-fardel a footback? ... It is otherwise now, for my very share in playing apparel will not be sold for £200." "Truly," said Roberto, "it is strange that you should so prosper in that vain practice, for that it seems to me that your voice is nothing gracious."'

The player does not take offence at this gibe, he has too good an opinion of himself. "I can serve to make a pretty speech, for I was a country author, passing at a moral ... and for seven years was absolute interpreter of the puppets." The episode ends with the player being able to engage Roberto, the needy scholar, to pen plays for him and to lodge him in a house of retail for the purpose.

That overlooked passage tells us several things. One suspicious circumstance is that seven-year apprenticeship: it was precisely seven years since Shakespeare's recorded appearance in Stratford in 1585 and this attack on him in London in 1592. We know that he had had a long, hard apprenticeship. We do not have to pay attention to the insulting reference about going on foot with his playing fardel on his back. In the Sonnets he is journeying on horseback, and we do know that the expensive attire of actors, their rich costumes, were a valuable part of their possessions, from their wills. Most important, this actor is a provincial, a countryman, neither a university man nor a Londoner, like almost all the leading figures in the theatre world. And he has a provincial accent.

That was familiar enough in the Elizabethan age – Sir Walter Ralegh 'spake broad Devonshire to his dying day.' People spoke according to their localities – and from Shakespeare's spellings, he spoke with the West Midlands accent of his native county.

We all know that he strongly resented this public attack on him, for he called on Henry Chettle, who had published it and now made a handsome apology: 'myself have seen his demeanour no less civil than he excellent in the quality he professes. Besides, divers of worship have reported his uprightness of dealing, which argues his honesty, and his facetious grace in writing that approves his art.' I know no such apology in the whole of that unapologetic age.

It is very well known; but few have noticed that Shakespeare refers to it in his indirect way in a sonnet that belongs precisely to the time – Sonnet 112, i.e. 1593:

> Your love and pity doth the impression fill
> Which vulgar scandal stamped upon my brow;
> For what care I who calls me well or ill,
> So you o'er-greene my bad, my good allow?

One needs to be subtle to track him in his work, he is no simple countryman; but *everything* about him, within his work and from outside, external as well as internal evidence, gives a completely consistent picture. No need for the confusion about our greatest writer:

I call it both contemptible, on the part of those responsible for it, and deplorable, in its effects upon the public.

I had nothing much new to add on the subject of *The Taming of the Shrew*, except two things. One was to firm up the date of it, which belongs to this time, 1593, and to underline its Cotswold background for the benefit of those who did not realise how well Shakespeare knew that neighbourhood. I had already pointed out that Warwickshire was given a good show in the *Henry VI* plays, and a Sir William Lucy, of nearby Charlecote, awarded a part.

Now, in the Induction to the *Shrew*, Christopher Sly comes from Barton-on-the-Heath, where Shakespeare's aunt and uncle, the Lamberts, lived. They had bought some of his mother's Arden inheritance when his father's affairs went down hill from 1576, when the schoolboy would be twelve (no university for him). Marion Hacket is referred to as 'the fat ale-wife of Wincot', a hamlet across the meadows south of Stratford. We know that there were Hackets thereabouts then, and that there were Slys in Stratford. I dared to point out how silly pedants had been to retain the misprint for 'old John Naps of *Greece*', when it referred to Greet, another hamlet across the Cotswolds, and persuaded my Yale friend to correct it in his edition of the play.

It pleased me also to bring home the social usages of the time. The Lord of the Induction gives instructions to take the players when they arrive 'to the buttery': nothing demeaning in that, but no doubt that would be where as a travelling actor Shakespeare would have been entertained often enough. The play reflects, in the luxurious entertainment Sly is to receive, the playwright's own increasing sophistication with his entrance into the Southampton circle. Some editors had seen in the rare use of the word 'proceeders', when proceeding, the term familiar to us at universities on stepping up to a degree. But no-one had connected this with the fact that the previous summer Southampton, a Cambridge man, had proceeded M.A. at Oxford. We shall see that it was likely that his poet was in attendance.

I inferred this from the passage in *A Midsummer Night's Dream* which describes trembling academics breaking down in the formidable presence of the Queen on her state visit:

> Where I have come, great clerks have purposèd
> To greet me with premeditated welcomes;
> Where I have seen them shiver and look pale,
> Make periods in the midst of sentences,
> Throttle their practised accents in their fears,
> And in conclusion dumbly have broke off.

It is so authentically visual – evidently, one would say, from some observant onlooker upon the scene.

Others had noticed the tribute to the Queen, Cupid aiming his dart

> At a fair Vestal, thronèd by the West . . .
> But I might see young Cupid's fiery shaft
> Quenched in the chaste beams of the watery moon:
> And the imperial Votaress passed on
> In maiden meditation, fancy-free.

They have suggested that this refers to the celebrated entertainment of the Queen by Leicester at Kenilworth in 1575. In those days the castle was half surrounded by a large lake. All the countryside flocked there to the week's entertainments. Literary critics would not know, however, their point: this was Leicester's last effort to persuade Elizabeth I to marry him. In vain: Cupid's dart was certainly quenched in the watery moon.

My particular contribution was to settle the date and circumstances of the play. We know from a reference in the Sonnets that Shakespeare had it in mind to tell a 'summer's story.' When we come to the end of the play we find it is Mayday and that the young lovers are returning from Maying. The elderly couple on their way to marriage are persons of state, the Duke and his Hippolyta.

Very well: Southampton's mother married her second husband, Sir Thomas Heneage, on the 2nd of May 1594. He was already elderly, and was very much a person of state, as Privy Councillor and Vice-Chamberlain. People have seen that the play was fitted to a wedding ceremony, a private one, and have made suggestions all over the place as to which one. Chambers cites half-a-dozen weddings over a decade, from 1590 to 1600, as if one were as good a conjecture as another. There is no reason for conjecture. This particular wedding was entirely private, and there is some indication that the Queen was displeased at it: Heneage was in disfavour that spring.

In the first scene the Duke speaks in disapprobation of the virgin state:

> To live a barren sister all your life! . . .
> But earthlier-happy is the rose distilled

(an image from the Sonnets of this date)

> Than that which, withering on the virgin thorn,
> Grows, lives, and dies in single blessedness.

It is hardly likely that the tactful author would have written those words for an occasion at which the Virgin Queen was to preside. Yet blinkered editors have specially picked out weddings graced by her presence. I said at the time that social sense should have told them otherwise.

More important was the new light to be thrown on *Romeo and Juliet* from the realisation of how close Shakespeare was to Southampton and in touch with events that concerned him. What turned his poet's mind to the new subject of a family feud, and finding a love-story with that as background or, rather, which dominated it? That was Shakespeare's way, as we have seen from the beginning, with *Henry VI* – something in events at the time suggested a subject. Nothing surprising in this: it is the way real writers write, particularly a dramatist with the nose for 'box-office appeal' and success which Greene had noticed in him.

In the country at Titchfield – the grand house which Southampton's grandfather had made out of the Abbey premises – the spoiled grandson was close friends with his Wiltshire neighbours, Charles and Henry Danvers of Dauntsey. The Danvers family were at bitter feud with the Longs of Wraxall: there had already been affrays and manslaughter among their retainers. The feud culminated with the Danvers faction breaking in upon the Longs at dinner at Corsham on 4 October 1594, when young Henry Danvers – Southampton's special friend – killed the son and heir of the Longs.

The brothers then fled to Titchfield, where Southampton gave them shelter in a lodge in the park, fed them, and spirited them away across Channel to serve under Henry of Navarre. In the hue-and-cry after them, 'Signor Florio, an Italian' threatened to throw the sheriff on the ferry across the Itchen overboard. In the play Lady Capulet is full of the spirit of revenge. We know from external documents that this was just like Lady Danvers, who had driven the feud on. John Aubrey, as a Wiltshire relation, knew all about it; he tells us that she was 'an Italian', meaning an Italianate type, 'of great wit and spirit, but revengeful.' The father's spirit was broken by it all – the affair made a sensation and caused great trouble. When he died, to obtain her sons' pardon Lady Danvers found it necessary, besides a large payment, to marry a younger son of Lord Chamberlain Hunsdon. We see how these things connect up, if we know enough about them and have the perception to see *how*. They consistently confirm and corroborate each other.

Shakespeare knew a suitable story to make use of in Arthur Brooke's dull *Romeus and Juliet*. Professor C.J. Sisson, a good authority, makes the revealing comment, 'it is notable that we see so little in Shakespeare of the prevailing attitude of his fellow dramatists towards Italy, which presents a land and people of Machiavellian villainy, of poison and assassination, the Circe of nations. Love, to his mind, was evidently the traffic of this enchanted city of Italy.' Well, we do not have far to look for the Italian colouring and sympathies, the scraps of the language, the reference to Petrarch – what with Emilia *and* Florio.

He made quite a different character of Mercutio from Brooke's conventional figure. Some people have seen Marlowe in Mercutio, and now that we know how close Shakespeare was to him – not only in writing *Venus and Adonis* in rivalry with *Hero and Leander* for Southampton's favour, but also in play-writing – we can say that they were right. Mercutio is no more in favour of the love of women than Marlowe was: they both preferred friendship with their own sex. Then too Mercutio was as quick on the draw as Marlowe was, who had been killed only a year or so before at the end of May 1593. One of Juliet's rapturous phrases echoes a typical passage from Marlowe's last play, *Edward II*; and it is appropriate that the finest passages of poetry are given to Mercutio.

No more – except that I noticed how the final *dénouement* of the play is brought about by the plague. Friar John could not deliver the crucial message to Romeo about Juliet being in a trance, because he was shut up on account of the plague; nor could they

get a messenger to bring it you,
So fearful were they of infection.

The plague had been all about them in those years 1592 and 1593,
the theatre folk especially affected by it, as we know from Edward
Alleyn's correspondence with Philip Henslowe.

The play then was written 1594–5.

Of *The Merchant of Venice* Professor Sisson writes, 'the whole picture
of Jewish thought, family life, religion, communal and racial feeling,
emerges for the first time in England.' How did William Shakespeare
come to know so much about it? – there were very few Jews in
Elizabethan England.

We now know the answer. Roger Prior has told us that the Bassanos
– the English called them Bassany – were Jewish; which makes Emilia
half-Jewish. No wonder she was something exceptional. We now
know that the playwright of the Southampton circle was a perfect
magpie for picking up information and making the most of it. Moreover, the case of Dr Lopez in 1594 – referred to in the Sonnets –
touched the circle closely; for it was Essex who ran the conceited
Jewish doctor to death, and Pérez lent a hand to exposing him as
the double agent he was. The Queen was convinced that he had
no intention of poisoning her, and held out against condemning him,
but could not resist the popular outcry. The affair made a great sensation. The Admiral's Company cashed in on it by reviving Marlowe's
The Jew of Malta. The newly formed Chamberlain's Company went
one better in every sense with *The Merchant of Venice*. Where Marlowe's Barabas is the usual stock-figure of a Jew, a comic caricature
for the mob, Shakespeare transcends that with human sympathy.
In the end one comes to sympathise with Shylock, much the most
interesting character in the play: this is borne out by its being sometimes referred to as 'The Jew of Venice'.

I was able to point up the contemporary background, though I
did not know that the Bassanos were Jewish. That was Roger Prior's
contribution: the reader can now see for himself how it confirms
my work. No-one has been able to urge a single consideration or
circumstance against the identification of Emilia Bassano. Professor
Prior has recently gone into the play from this point of view, with

a close study of the word-play, puns etc, though the identification does not need this reinforcement: it is already clear on every ground.

I pointed out how authentically London stood for the picture of Venice, with the merchants

> Plucking the grass to know where sits the wind,
> Peering in maps for ports and piers and roads.

It is exactly like the picture we get from Forman's case-books, with the merchants coming to him to know the prospects for their argosies. Other contemporary touches too were brought out.

> As, after some oration fairly spoken
> By a belovèd prince, there does appear
> Among the buzzing, pleasèd multitude,
> Where every something being blent together
> Turns to a wild of nothing, save of joy.

Evidently the observant actor had observed the great actress of the age, always playing to the gallery: she was an eloquent orator, with her high, rather shrill authoritative voice.

And the dating of the play too: there is a reference to

> my wealthy *Andrew* docked in sand,
> Vailing her high top lower than her ribs.

At Essex's capture of Cadiz in 1596 the galleon *St Andrew* had been run aground; when being brought up-Channel she was nearly wrecked. In the play Antonio's ship is reported as wrecked on the Goodwin Sands. Francis Meres mentions the play in 1598; so its date is clear – 1596–7.

In *As You Like It* how could anyone miss the striking reference to Marlowe,

> Dead shepherd, now I find thy saw of might –
> 'Who ever loved that loved not at first sight?'

It is the only time that Shakespeare quotes a specific line from a contemporary, virtually by name. The phrase 'dead shepherd' too is touching, for 'shepherd' is the word by which poets recognised a fellow poet. Phrases from Marlowe are echoed throughout Shakespeare's work, especially the earlier; and I have cited the cross-references between *Venus and Adonis* and *Hero and Leander*, which show that the rival poets were perfectly aware of each other's work.

This is not the only reference to Marlowe in this play – there are several. Why? The answer is that in the year 1598 Marlowe's unfinished *Hero and Leander* was at length published. This brought him and his work back to Shakespeare's suggestible mind, always ready to respond to whatever was in the news. So we find,

> Leander, he would have lived many a fair year though Hero had turned nun, if it had not been for a hot midsummer night. For, good youth, he went but forth to wash him in the Hellespont and, being taken with the cramp, was drowned.

As for Marlowe himself:

> when a man's verses cannot be understood ... it strikes a man more dead *than a great reckoning in a little room.*

The 'great reckoning in a little room' referred to the house at Deptford where Marlowe had been killed in a quarrel over 'le reckoning', as the coroner's inquest reported.

Shakespeare would have known all about that – and that was all there was to it. Everybody knew Marlowe's quarrelsome temper, especially when drunk – he and his acquaintance had been drinking there all day. He had been involved in affrays before; and in my *Christopher Marlowe* I had been able to include a new unknown reference to him on a last visit to Canterbury, his home town, when he was involved in a scuffle outside a tavern, with a musician, William Corkine.[1]

When Professor Hotson discovered the inquest giving the circumstances of Marlowe's death, he wanted to suggest that there was more to it than was in it. Simply because some years before Walsingham had sent Marlowe to Rheims to report on what the Catholic exiles were up to there. I advised Hotson at the time that it would be a mistake to suggest anything more, for which there was no evidence – we knew well enough what Marlowe was like: he would have come to a sticky end some time or other.

Hotson took that without demur in those early years; but in all his subsequent work he went beyond the evidence, trying to make out something more than was there. He became more and more

[1] v. my *Christopher Marlowe* (paperback edition), 213–14.

erratic, departing from the common sense of the documents into the realm of fantasy.

In the play Rosalind, disguised as a youth, takes the name Ganymede; in Marlowe's *Dido* Ganymede is depicted as dandled on Jove's knee, to Juno's disgust. Marlowe was devoutly homosexual, and homosexuality appears in all his works – in contrast to Shakespeare, so keen on women.

Other topical references were obvious to the historian. To Rosalind learning about Orlando is a 'South Sea of discovery'. To the Elizabethans the Pacific was the South Sea, being discovered. Rosalind's love 'has an unknown bottom, like the Bay of Portugal', familiar but then unplumbed. She will 'weep for nothing, like Diana in the fountain.' The fountain with a statue of Diana, 'water prilling from her naked breast', had recently been set up in Cheapside, familiar tramping-ground to Shakespeare lodging close by at this time in Bishopsgate.

Most important is the way his country background is made use of: the Forest of Arden, his own Warwickshire background and folk, shepherds and sheepcotes, valley bottoms and streams bordered with osiers. A poor vicar's name, Martext, reflects the Marprelate Tracts coming out at the time. We can leave the literary references, Thomas Lodge and Sidney, to Eng. Lit. people: they are well enough known.

What they did not know was the importance of Arden, his mother's name and family, to the son. For the Ardens of Park Hall were Warwickshire gentry, and Mary Arden's father of Wilmcote was something more than a farmer. Now well-established and successful in the theatre, having purchased about the best property in his native town, William proceeded to take out a coat-of-arms – to Ben Jonson's mockery. He took it out in his father's name, so that himself would have been born a gentleman. The grant from Garter King of Arms tells us that this was for John Shakespeare's 'late grandfather's faithful and valiant service', for which he had been advanced and rewarded by Henry VII. We know nothing about this – was somebody telling a tall tale? Robert Arden, William's grandfather, is described as 'esquire', which he was not; neither was William, who was merely a 'gent'. Three years later he made an attempt to quarter his arms with those of the Ardens of Park Hall. This was disallowed, and even the original grant of arms was criticised.

These things may appear of no importance to people who know nothing of Elizabethan society and how important they were at the time. But they show that Shakespeare was proud rather of his Arden inheritance and wanted to make something of it. That again is completely consistent with all that we have discovered about him, and corroborates it.

5

The History Plays and Contemporary Life

It was not unreasonable to suppose that the Elizabethan historian might have some light to throw on the History plays, in particular lighting up the contemporary scene as reflected in them. All the more so since Shakespeare is the most historically minded of all our dramatists. More than a third of his work is historical: ten plays on English history, four on classical history, Roman and Greek, two on the pre-history of Britain, *Cymbeline* and *King Lear*. With the Elizabethans pre-history was hardly distinguished from authentic history, as we see from Holinshed, Camden or Carew. *Macbeth* is based on Scottish history; there is some historical background for *Hamlet*, ultimately coming from Saxo Grammaticus. And there is an indeterminate historical background for *Titus Andronicus*, *Pericles* and *Timon of Athens*.

The fact is obvious, but again no-one had paid much attention to it or seen the significance of it. Yet Shakespeare's mind was profoundly *historical*; his imagination was set alight by events of the past. Not by the future, Utopian dreams like those of superficial writers, Shaw or Wells. The future may appeal to doctrinaire prose minds, but not to the poetic imagination. It is arguable that Shaw's best play is *St Joan*, that Shelley's best is *The Cenci*, and Tolstoy's *War and Peace*, certainly not his deluded writings about the future. Similarly with Scott and Balzac: their best works are about the past, if in their case the immediate past, a generation or so before them.

In Shakespeare's case the exciting events of the previous century

– the war in France, the Wars of the Roses between Lancaster and York, all the way from Richard II to Richard III, appealed specially to him. Of course they provided ready subjects for plays, and were popular with the Elizabethan public, which had plenty of excitements in its own time. But Shakespeare did not deal with these topicalities, as Ben Jonson, for example, did. Shakespeare's was not that kind of mind, journalistically keen on current events. His was a romantic mind, poetic in its marrow. The difference was noted at the time. Jonson's historical plays, *Catiline* and *Sejanus* are dead; his contemporary plays, *The Alchemist*, which reflects something of 'Dr' Forman, and *Volpone* very much alive.

All the same Shakespeare naturally reflects the world about him, as an exceptionally acute observer would – often quite directly, but as it were in an aside, almost casually. Again, as in his personal references, apart from direct autobiography in the Sonnets, his touch is often indirect, oblique, glancing. It is sometimes a subtle matter to catch it; one needs historical knowledge plus perception to light things up four centuries and more later.

We must then concentrate on this aspect, how the contemporary scene is reflected – if not wholly; for there remains how Shakespeare regarded history, since he was so keen on it. His mind was so geared to it that a professional medievalist of our time, K. B. McFarlane, has described him, if with some exaggeration, as the greatest of historians.

History as such was not taught in Elizabethan schools: everything was based on Latin, especially grammar and rhetoric. So ancient history came in on a side-wind from the classics, and Elizabethans were better acquainted with it than with later times. Hence modern and medieval history had to them the excitement of novelty. Ancient names, like Julius Caesar or Alexander, Cato or Brutus, were more familiar to them than Norman, Robert or William; and those names came readily to mind from the Latin literature they read.

We may suppose that the prentice-piece, *Titus Andronicus*, with its echoes from Seneca and Ovid, Shakespeare may have brought up with him from the country, since it is full of vivid country strokes – deer-hunting especially – that go incongruously with the gory subject. But it was with the *Henry VI* trilogy that the player turned playwright found himself – and his public. What an Elizabethan historian with his nose on the scent would notice is this:

> One would have lingering wars with little cost;
> Another would fly swift but wanteth wings;
> A third thinks, without expense at all,
> By guileful fair words peace may be obtained.

This exactly represented the current attitudes to the war with Spain. Younger activists, like Essex and Ralegh, were in favour of pushing forward the war at all costs or without counting the cost. The third course was that favoured by the Queen, sensible woman: 'guileful fair words . . . without expense.' Precisely right up to the sailing of the Armada she was negotiating with Parma in the Netherlands for peace.

What the Netherlands were to Spain, Ireland was to the Elizabethans, a continual worry and expense. They could never disengage themselves from the neighbouring island for strategic reasons, apart from anything else: it would be occupied by the enemy. They hoped rather to lick it into shape, *their* shape. They were genuinely shocked by a society in large part even pre-medieval: septs subsisting on nomadic herds of cattle, constant tribal infighting, mutual killings like those that disgraced the O'Neils of Ulster; the oppressive rule of the great chiefs that bore hardly upon lesser folk, with their demands to support war-bands, kern and gallowglass. All Elizabethan writing, as well as reports from the island, show that the English were horrified. They wanted to see the other island with a settled society after the model of England: lords and gentry, squires and parsons ruling civilised towns and villages. Celts, however – though not all of them – preferred their own way of life, differenced by language and religion.

Echoes of what was going on in Ireland are to be heard in all the early plays, until its subjugation at the end of the reign. In *2 Henry VI* a post arrives,

> To signify that rebels there are up
> And put the Englishmen unto the sword.
> Send succours, lords, and stop the rage betime
> Before the wound do grow incurable.

We hear of the 'uncivil kerns of Ireland': this meant 'not reduced to civility', as the English wished. 'Gallowglass' are the warrior following of tribal chieftains; this applied to the Hebrides as to Northern

Ireland, which were in a comparable state of civilisation, enjoying mutual amenities, feuds and massacres. Shakespeare shared the normal English attitude towards it all, with none of the sympathy which he extended towards the Welsh – with whom, at Stratford not far from the Severn, he was familiar.

> The uncivil kerns of Ireland are in arms
> And temper clay with blood of Englishmen.
> To Ireland will you lead a band of men,
> Collected choicely, from each county some.

This was exactly how it was done. In the critical 1590s a draft was imposed upon each western county to send bands for service in Ireland.

In *Richard II* we read,

> The lining of his coffers shall make coats
> To deck our soldiers for these Irish wars.

Exact again: these bands were provided with 'coat-and-conduct' money: to clothe them and conduct them from western ports for transport.

In *2 Henry VI* we find the image,

> like a shag-haired crafty kern
> Hath he conversèd with the enemy.

Again, in *Richard II*:

> We must supplant those rough, rug-headed kerns.

This refers to the Irish 'glibs', long hair over the eyes, which made disguise so easy: hence it was forbidden by statute to wear them. Another feature of Irish warfare is recalled in:

> You rode like a kern of Ireland, your French hose off and in your strait strossers –

i.e. breeks; they rode without stirrups.

When we come to *Macbeth* the common Gaelic culture of Hebrides and Ulster appears:

> the merciless Macdonald,
> Worthy to be a rebel . . .
> from the Western Isles
> Of kerns and gallowglasses is supplied.

Enough of these references: the primitive background across the Irish seas is clear.

The struggle in Ireland reached its climax in the last years of the reign, 1598–1603, when the resistance of Ulster found a notable leader in the last native prince, Hugh O'Neil. He inflicted a heavy defeat upon English arms in 1598. Next year an army was sent under Essex to meet the danger. Essex was always popular, and was given a grand send-off from London – as described in *Henry V*.

> How London doth pour out her citizens!
> The mayor and all his brethren in best sort –
> Like to the senators of antique Rome,
> With the plebeians swarming at their heels,
> Go forth and fetch their conquering Caesar in.
>
> – As by a lower but loving likelihood
> Were now the General of our gracious Empress,
> As in good time he may, from Ireland coming,
> Bringing rebellion broachèd on his sword,
> How many would the peaceful city quit
> To welcome him!

Everybody has been able to recognise this clear reference to Essex's departure in 1599. Then why not recognise other, less obvious, references when pointed out by someone familiar with events at the time?

We can, in fact, follow a revealing graph in Shakespeare's changing attitude towards Essex, as he went along his dizzy course to disaster, taking Southampton with him. Shakespeare was close to it all: as an earlier member of Southampton's circle, this was his affiliation – the group that had his personal affections, in opposition to the Cecils and Ralegh. From frequent appearances at Court he was in a privileged position to know what was going on there, and hear what was being said, while remaining uncommitted. No better position for a dedicated observer, and a prudent one, never making a rash step (unlike Marlowe and Ben Jonson).

Hence we may trace the graph, with Essex's regular cult of popularity echoed in the portrayal of Bolingbroke in *Richard II*:

> You would have thought the very windows spake –
> So many greedy looks of young and old
> Through casements darted their desiring eyes
> Upon his visage . . .
> Whilst he, from one side to the other turning
> Bare-headed, lower than his proud steed's neck

> Bespake them thus, 'I thank you, countrymen.'

This was always Essex's way: we do not know historically that it was Bolingbroke's. Here is Essex again:

> Ourself . . .
> Observed his courtship of the common people:
> How he did seem to dive into their hearts
> With humble and familiar courtesy:
> What reverence he did throw away on slaves
> Wooing poor craftsmen with the craft of smiles . . .
> Off goes his bonnet to an oyster-wench;
> A brace of draymen bid God speed him well,
> And had the tribute of his supple knee
> With 'Thanks, my countrymen, my loving friends.'
> As were our England in reversion his,
> And he our subjects' next degree in hope.

This is Richard II speaking, from the monarch's point of view, the play written about 1595 – before Essex became a challenge to Elizabeth I in her last years.

By the time we come to *Much Ado About Nothing*, of 1599, we find the most sensitive register of the time noting,

> like favourites,
> Made proud by princes, that advance their pride
> Against that power that bred it.

This is precisely what was happening. Essex had been spoiled by the Queen when he was young, and now he was advancing to challenge her authority. She distrusted his cult of popularity, as well she might, detracting from her own; he was now going on to a direct confrontation, as no one else dared to do. Still he remained the most dazzling figure at Court, beloved by the people:

> The courtier's, soldier's, scholar's, eye, tongue, sword,
> The expectancy and rose of the fair state,
> The glass of fashion and the mould of form,
> The observed of all observers.

This is 1600, with *Hamlet*. There are flecks, and perhaps more, of Essex in Hamlet – but in Shakespeare's oblique way, all put back into a story from the remote past, and in a foreign country. Note too, that what the play hinges upon is the succession to the throne – the subject that was in everybody's mind. Shakespeare regularly picked up what was happening at the time. There is in Hamlet Essex's brilliancy, and also his hesitancy, his long halting before making his final throw. 'The courtier's, soldier's, scholar's, eye, tongue, sword', precisely: Essex was well educated and eloquent, in addition to everything else, his letters show how well, even poetically he wrote.

Dover Wilson rightly saw this; and to his credit he saw the plain reference to the siege of Ostend, which was the chief war news at the time:[1]

> We go to gain a little patch of ground
> That hath in it no profit but the name.

The ding-dong struggle for Ostend went on for two or three years and consumed the lives of thousands of men.

> To my shame I see
> The imminent death of twenty thousand men
> That, for a fantasy and trick of fame
> Go to their graves like beds, fight for a plot
> Whereon the numbers cannot try the cause,
> Which is not tomb enough and Continent
> To hide the slain.

That is increasingly what William Shakespeare thought about war as it went drearily on. So did the Queen, and so – more interestingly from our point of view – did Falstaff. He was not one for fighting, any more than his creator was.

And, of course, Polonius has more than flecks of old Lord Burghley, with his Precepts and his prosiness. It was safe to caricature him now, for he had died in 1598. He had been the chief obstacle in the way for Essex and his party, and he had been irremovable. After his death the faction-fighting became more bitter, with his son, Robert Cecil, taking his place. Essex's outbreak into the city in February 1601, with the object of an attack on Whitehall, was fatal. He had been spurred on by Southampton. Both were condemned to death, Southampton's sentence suspended, while he languished in the Tower until the Queen's death.

The closeness of the theatre to current events is brought home to us by this. The day before the outbreak a group of Essex's followers went across river to the 'Globe', and got the players to put on *Richard II*, to put people in mind of a monarch's deposition. The Queen was well aware of this, for she said to William Lambarde later that

---

[1] Chambers, typically, would not have it to be.

year: 'I am Richard II. Know ye not that?' She went on, 'this tragedy was played forty times in open streets and houses.' No doubt this was an exaggeration; but the deposition scene was censored from being printed until James I had safely succeeded to the throne.

However, when Elizabeth I died, her favourite playwright was not among those who paid an obituary tribute to her. Not until many years had elapsed did he do that in *Henry VIII*.

There is no difficulty in detecting reflections upon these striking events in *Troilus and Cressida*, in all probability a private play, shortly after. Nor, more important, an atmosphere of disillusionment, accents of personal bitterness entering into the themes of war and politics, love and betrayal. Along with this we are struck, in the speeches of wise Ulysses, with Shakespeare's emphatic affirmation of the necessity of social order, of duty and obedience, everyone taking his proper place in society according to function; the anarchy that ensues when this is undermined and overthrown.

Shakespeare's was always a conservative view of society. A member of the governing class, a gentleman (unlike the riff-raff of Bohemia), he shared the government's view. But his personal affiliations were with his friends in the opposition. There is no more embittering experience in politics than to see one's own party and friends acting like a lot of fools and heading straight for the rocks. This is what he witnessed from close at hand: the bitterness of it went into *Troilus and Cressida*. It has a cynical temper quite unlike him, but the reflections on what had passed are unmistakable.

> Things small as nothing, for request's sake only,
> He makes important: possessed he is with greatness,
> And speaks not to himself but with a pride
> That quarrels at self-breath.

That had been Essex's way all along: regularly putting pressure on the Queen for concessions, appointments for his friends, building up his faction; then, when denied, sulking, and withdrawing from Court.

> He is so plaguy-proud that the death tokens of it
> Cry 'No recovery.'

He had gone too far, exploited his favour beyond endurance, and was responsible for his own fall. The consequences are reflected in the play:

> 'Tis certain greatness, once fallen out with fortune,
> Must fall out with men too: what the declined is
> He shall as soon read in the eyes of others
> As feel in his own fall . . .
> Which, when they fell, as being slippery standers . . .
> Do pluck down another, and together die in the fall.

Many had been involved with Essex in the catastrophe, most notably Southampton. Others crossed over, but one notability deserted him before the event, when he saw the headlong course Essex was taking. In *Hamlet* we find,

> The great man down, you mark his favourite flies,
> The poor advanced makes friends of enemies.

This is precisely what Francis Bacon did. Essex had pushed hard for his preferment. We need not blame Bacon for ratting from a sinking ship (what are rats supposed to do – line up on the bridge with the captain?). He crossed over to seek favour with Essex's enemy, Robert Cecil; and was generally blamed for taking a prominent part in Essex's trial. Fortunately no such choice presented itself to an observer on the sidelines – no politician on the make, a mere playwright.

The fall of that luminary from the skies left a sad gap. Essex's execution, though politically necessary, was unpopular; the people cherished his memory, and sang ballads to it. The Queen herself suffered from the strain of it all, and plodded sadly on. There was a queasiness, a sickness in the air, weariness with the long war, disillusion, anxiety about the succession and what would happen upon her demise. Something of all this is reflected in the plays of these years: *Hamlet, Troilus and Cressida, All's Well That Ends Well*.

Of Essex's career Shakespeare was a close observer, as with Southampton, so no wonder its rise and fall may be traced graphically in the plays. This has led us ahead of the early 1590s, to which *Richard III* belongs. It follows closely upon the heels of the *Henry VI* trilogy, about 1592. The play offers no problems, and I had little to contribute, except to emphasise how close to the tradition Shakespeare was in his depiction of the King – hero is not quite the word for him. Naturally the dramatist made him more of an histrionic, even amusing, character than Richard III was historically. Though historians know a good deal about him, he was far from amusing. He appears to have been a good soldier, and might have made a competent king, if he had not been murderer of his nephews. That was what turned the stomach of the country against him, lost him the support of most of his own party, and let in the unknown, but respectable, Lancastrian claimant.

Shakespeare's portrait derives in good part from Sir Thomas More, who was in a position to know about Richard's *coup d'état*. For More was a friend of Norfolk who, as Earl of Surrey, was in the room at the Tower when Richard haled his brother Edward IV's chief friend, Lord Hastings, out to summary execution. After that there was no turning back – as Richard says in the play, he was so far *in*. More had known FitzJames, later bishop of London, and others who were on the spot; his own father, Sir John More, had been a young lawyer watching in the city at the time.

Everybody knew, though they did not know *how*. It was Sir Thomas More's business as the ablest of lawyers and a man dedicated to truth, to ferret things out. We all know that. But I was able to show that, less than ten years before the play, a new source of information appeared. Lord Henry Howard's *Defensative Against Supposed Prophecies*, 1583, gives us the Howards' family tradition as to Richard's 'heinous crime'. They were a Yorkist family and owed their dukedom to Richard.

We need not waste time on the nonsense that occasionally crops up – that Richard was as innocent as a new-born babe, that the crime was committed by anybody other than he. One critic of my book *Bosworth Field and the Wars of the Roses* wrote that Richard had no motive to do it! – when he had all the motive in the world: to make himself king in place of his nephew. The two boys were never seen again after August 1483, when the order for their murder issued from Warwick Castle, where we know independently that Richard then was.

All that is relevant here is to enforce that William Shakespeare understood the springs of human action, ambition, ruthlessness, crime better than crackpots who do not qualify to hold an opinion, least of all on historic events centuries ago. Shakespeare was not far removed in time from those events: Elizabeth I herself was but the grand-daughter of the man who gave Richard his come-uppance at Bosworth.

It is all like the nonsense about Shakespeare not having written his own plays, or the obscurantism that refuses to recognise who the Dark Lady was, when her identity has been made clear beyond dispute. It all comes under the same heading – people's inability to *think*.

A few things needed to be said about *King John*, to relate it to its time and the playwright's own experience. First as to dating, about which there had been much argument. We have an indication from this:

> So, by a roaring tempest on the flood,
> A whole armado of convicted [concerted] sail
> Is scattered and disjoined from fellowship.

This is precisely what happened to the second armada, of 1596, which was dispersed by storms before it reached the English coast. The play would have been written that autumn or winter.

In spite of the subject giving opportunity for Protestant rant against the Papacy, as in John Bale's earlier play, the tactful dramatist does not make that appeal to the gallery. (Remember, too, that Southampton was a Catholic.) The appeal is all to patriotism. We are given some anti-French sentiment, particularly highlighting French inconsistency and their breaking of oaths. This reflected the bad impression made by Henry of Navarre's desertion of the Protestant cause, which was in mind too in *Love's Labour's Lost*.

Shakespeare's reaction to all this is to be seen in the famous exordium about Commodity, i.e. political expediency:

> That smooth-faced gentleman, tickling Commodity,
> Commodity, the bias of the world –
> The world, who of itself is peizèd [poised] well . . .
> Till this advantage, this vile-drawing bias,
> This sway of motion, this Commodity
> Makes it take head from all indifferency [impartiality] . . .
> Since kings break faith upon Commodity.

Touches of his native Stratford appear in this faithful townsman's work:

> I saw a smith stand with his hammer – thus,
> The whilst his iron did on the anvil cool,
> With open mouth swallowing a tailor's news:
> Who, with his shears and measure in his hand,
> Standing on slippers, which his nimble haste
> Had falsely drawn upon contrary feet.

It is a speaking vignette, a scene the writer would have beheld. Edgar Fripp, the admirable custodian of the Birthplace, who knew Shakespeare's Stratford better than anyone, is able to tell us that in Henley Street at the time was Hornby's smithy, while next to it the cottages were owned by tailor Wedgewood.[1]

That August Shakespeare's only boy Hamnet (the name is interchangeable with Hamlet) died; and so we find,

> Grief fills the room up of my absent child,
> Lies in his bed, walks up and down with me,
> Puts on his pretty looks, repeats his words,
> Remembers me of all his gracious parts,
> Stuffs out his vacant garments with his form.

The personal feeling is unmistakable in this, to anyone who knows how poetry gets written. And again, in the mother's question whether

> we shall see and know our friends in heaven:
> If that be true, I shall see my boy again.

I too have been asked just that question by a grieving mother.

The massive Chambers could recognise no personal feeling here. 'The sentimentalism of commentators is apt to find in the play a reflection of the natural sorrow of the poet at the death of his own son Hamnet.'[2] The boy Arthur's tragedy is the most moving part of the play – and also the most intimately *felt*. However, the authoritative (and authoritarian) scholar goes on dismissively: 'the sentimentalist is a dangerous leader in the slippery ways of literary biography. The grief of Constance rings true enough; but after all, her hint [!] of woe is common, and it must certainly not be assumed that a dramatist can only convince by reproducing those emotions which he has seen at play in his own household. It is safest to regard the tragic figure of the weeping mother as based rather upon broad human sympathies than upon personal experience.'

[1] E. J. Fripp, *Shakespeare's Stratford*, 16.
[2] E. K. Chambers, *Shakespeare: A Survey*, 97.

All that needs to be said about that is that the scholar-bureaucrat did not know how real writers are impelled to write. Nor was this the only case in which Sir Edmund got a human subject wrong: he was equally wrong about Sir Thomas Malory and Arthur of Britain. He was better writing about institutions, companies and stage history than about human beings.

Edgar Fripp, though apt to go too far in conjectures, knew immeasurably more about Shakespeare's Stratford than Chambers did. Just as Charlotte Stopes knew more about Warwickshire than the grandees who were so supercilious about her work. She was the first person to see that Mr W. H. must have been Southampton's step-father, Sir William Harvey. Though she did not know that the fact that knights at the time were addressed as Mr confirmed it.

With the two parts of *King Henry IV* we come to the masterpiece among the English History Plays. Shakespeare was the effectual inventor of the *genre*, with the mingling of historical characters with invented. This too was the ultimate source of the historical novel, with its extraordinary expansion from Scott's time to Europe, Russia, the United States, where it is still going today – notably with Gore Vidal.

These plays provide a notorious example of direct confrontation between literary and historical judgment, over the character of Prince Hal and the Rejection of Falstaff. So far from us being sentimentalists, *pace* Chambers, it is the literary folk who have been sentimentalists about both the character of the Prince and his almighty snub to his old crony, Falstaff.

Henry as king *had* to dissociate himself, publicly and privately, from the old reprobate. One could not have the country left open, let alone governed, by his announced intentions of thievery and corruption, promoting his kind. He had to be discountenanced. Not to see that betrays the usual lack of political judgment in literary critics such as Hazlitt (the Radical who had a cult of Napoleon, a military dictator!). Shakespeare, as usual, knew better. One of the main contributions of my original biography was to bring out how exceptional was his *political* understanding. Historians, from their subject and training, are in a better way to understand that.

In our time has emerged new information about Prince Hal's early years to confirm Shakespeare's picture of his giddy ways. Victorian critics did not know about this: once more Shakespeare was much closer to sources of information, as with Richard III. However, he did not know that, on the night of Henry IV's death, his son – taking on the burdens which had killed his father – spent the whole night in Westminster Abbey in confession with an anchorite. A medieval man, he seems to have undergone a conversion. No more pranks and games; he remained chaste thenceforward to his (political) marriage with Catherine of France. All was politics with him, as with his father – necessarily so, if they were to do their duty and maintain the throne and social order.

Richard II had been incapable of that, and so he had to go. Not to see that is the real sentimentality – there were sentimentalists at the time who did not see it. Of course it was a *personal* tragedy, and it had dire consequences. There was a sad irony in it too, which Shakespeare would not have known: Richard and the boy Henry were fonder of each other than the father and son were. Such is life, and such are the strains of high politics, of political necessity, upon the human heart. Henry IV and his son *were* rather cold at heart – and needed to be. They were successful kings.

Shakespeare enforces these lessons of social order, duty, obedience throughout his plays. A conservative man, a civilised humane man, he enforces again and again that undermining social order only brings about more suffering and worse cruelties than before. We have had plenty of reason to observe how true that is, in the revolutions of our own time everywhere – Europe, Russia, China, Africa, Central and South America. Shakespeare's view, as usual, has universal application.

Moreover, his view is a just one, not simply a reactionary one. The judgment holds good for kings and rulers, no less than for peoples: he had no illusions about either. If kings fall down on their duty, show themselves incapable of ruling, they have to go: witness Richard II and Henry VI. Crimes condemn them, as with Richard III. In the Wars of the Roses it was accepted that one killed one's enemies, but not children. Antony sacrificed half the Roman world for his infatuation for Cleopatra. It is the politic Octaviuses who win: Shakespeare's judgment told him that, though his heart was more with Antony.

The medieval historian K. B. McFarlane found out about Prince

Henry's riotousness when young. However, before depicting those roistering scenes Shakespeare saved the dignity of the king he would later portray, with the excuse:

> I know you all, and will awhile uphold
> The unyoked humour of your idleness . . .

Then, when he throws off 'this loose behaviour . . . my reformation shall show more goodly.' We know that, historically, it did have that effect. Some royal personages have failed through being too royal, and not knowing what ordinary people are like. Prince Hal learned early what they are.

And what of Falstaff?

Here there is an original point to be made – namely how much of Shakespeare there is in Falstaff – not only the sheer verbal brilliancy but how far did Falstaff express Shakespeare's point of view? Falstaff was not a fighting man; he thought that all the talk about 'honour' – to which the bastard-chivalry of the age was addicted and led so many good men to their deaths in duels, affrays and such – was largely wind, a puff of air, a word, 'a mere scutcheon'. William Shakespeare too was one for keeping out of trouble.

No illusions about Courts and their gaudy denizens either. This conservative mind regularly depicts Courts as slippery places, full of falsity, false friends, cut-throat rivalries, affectation. Here is a courtier:

> He was perfumèd like a milliner,
> And twixt his finger and his thumb he held
> A pouncet-box, which ever and anon
> He gave his nose and took't away again.

It might stand for the contemporary Earl of Oxford, a pansy, fantastic, with his Italian airs and ways, who preferred his Italian boy to his wife (Burghley's daughter) whom he treated abominably – and, wasting the whole of his inheritance, ended up as a pauper pensioner.

It is known that for Falstaff Shakespeare had the name of the fifteenth-century Sir John Fastolf to go on: it occurs to me that the medieval pronunciation of the name would have been more like Falstaff – misplacing of an 'l' in pronunciation is common enough, easier to say.

Now for what is revealing in the background. In the first of the two plays Falstaff is making for Coventry: 'we'll to Sutton Co'fil tonight', evidently the local pronunciation of Sutton Coldfield. But he will not disgrace the noble city of Coventry by marching his mouldy recruits through it. Another local pronunciation appears in Daintry for Daventry. Much more of the immediate Stratford background appears in the Second Part. We hear of Goodman Puff of Barson: this is how Barcheston was pronounced, where the famous Sheldon tapestries were woven. Local names appear: Perkes is common enough, but apparently there were Visors, a rare name, in the neighbourhood. The Cotswold place-name, Dumbleton, is used for a person; Hinckley is not far from the Warwickshire border. And so on.

This passage too is revealing:

> When we mean to build
> We first survey the plot, then draw the model.

It goes on to say that we 'must rate the cost of the erection' and, if too much, we decide on a 'new model' and 'fewer offices'. The now established dramatist, with the security of the Chamberlain's Company behind him, was able to buy handsome, five-gabled New Place – very grand of him – and was making repairs there, as we know independently. But this was beneath Sir Edmund Chambers' notice.

On *Henry V* Dover Wilson, who was not insensitive to history, has a very proper comment: 'a play which men of action have been wont silently to admire, and literary men, at any rate during the last 130 years, volubly to contemn.' So much the worse for the literary men: it shows up their lack of imagination. Dover Wilson had imagination – rather too much when it came to textual matters; but at least he had patriotism and knew what action demands. He had served at the Front in the First German War, 1914–18. Again, in the Second, at the time of the liberation of Europe from their hideous domination, we were thrilled and inspired to have *Henry V* brought on stage and film – as the Elizabethans were to see 'brave Talbot' in *Henry VI*.

After the send-off Essex got in 1599 the Chorus apologises for the inadequacy of the stage, 'this unworthy scaffold', to represent the war:

> Can this cockpit hold
> The vasty fields of France? Or may we cram
> Within this wooden O the very casques
> That did affright the air at Agincourt?

In 1599 the Lord Chamberlain's Company, of which Shakespeare was a founder member, took the wooden timbers of their 'Theatre' across the Thames and built the grander 'Globe'. 'This wooden O' is evidently the 'Globe', henceforth to be the permanent home of the Company, then the first in London, the Admiral's (for which Marlowe had written) taking second place.

The Chorus, who speaks before each Act, has a distinctly personal note. There is this author's regular flattering of the audience and beseeching its favour – such a contrast to Ben Jonson!

> But pardon, gentles all,
> The flat unraisèd spirits that hath dared
> On this unworthy scaffold to bring forth
> So great an object.

And then,

> Admit me Chorus to this history,
> Who, prologue-like, your humble patience pray,
> Gently to hear, kindly to judge our play.

Again, before Act III, he appeals to the imagination of the audience:

> Still be kind,
> And eke out our performance with your mind.

Before Act IV:

> Yet sit and see,
> Minding true things by what their mockeries be.

Notice that the courteous appeal is to the audience that *sits*, not to the groundlings standing in the pit. Finally, the Epilogue has an unmistakably autobiographical accent:

> Thus far, with rough and all unable pen, [!]
> Our bending author hath pursued the story.

The author himself is bowing to the audience, and, referring to the sad sequel of Henry VI,

Which oft our stage hath shown.

Here I made the suggestion that, in performances of *Henry V*, the opportunity should be taken to present the Chorus as the author himself. No notice of this suggestion has so far been taken.

With regard to the audience at least, the conventional professors have been put in their place. At Harvard the chief potentate in his time was Professor Harbage, who wrote what was regarded as the standard work on *Shakespeare's Audience*. Its assumption was conventionally democratic. The audience was 'motley, and for this we must be thankful. An audience so mixed compelled the most discerning of all authors to address himself to men and not to their badges, to men's intelligence and not to its levels. The influence upon the individual exerted by Class, whether high or low, is a cramping influence, warping the sympathies, prejudicing the mind. But where all classes are there is no class; there is that common humanity which subtends all. To the kind of audience for which he wrote, and to the fact that he did write for it, we owe Shakespeare's universality.'[1]

We see how muffish this is: anyone would think that the audience wrote the plays, and that Shakespeare's universality came from it.

This democratic assumption was overthrown by a young researcher going into the facts and figures, in Ann Jennalie Cook's, *The Privileged Playgoers of Shakespeare's London*. She showed that 'far from reflecting a cross-section of society, the spectators came chiefly from the upper levels of the social order ... The necessity for disproportionately large numbers of the privileged [i.e. gentry and professional classes] to be in London, supplied the dramatic companies with a loyal, lucrative audience. It was an audience that did not have to be lured into playgoing. The privileged had long fostered the drama as schoolboys [and at university], as patrons, and even as playwrights themselves. They enjoyed exclusive performances at Court, and in their own mansions. Always regarded as the chief clientèle of the small private theatres, the privileged probably dominated the huge public theatre audiences as well.'[2]

All this is only common sense, apart even from the statistics which

[1] A. Harbage, *Shakespeare's Audience*, 162.
[2] A. J. Cook, lib. cit., 8–9.

underwrite it: those people came to the theatres who could afford it, i.e. from the middle and upper classes. Those were the people who filled the galleries, and *sat*: theirs was the money that made the profits for the Companies and kept the theatres going, with additional returns from Court performances, where the audience was aristocratic. The pennies of the groundlings did not make the theatres pay, and they were a small minority of the audience.

Miss Cook's starting-point was to use 'the work of social historians to shed new light on Renaissance drama. The insights of the historians are, by and large, not well known to those working in Renaissance drama.' So far from wishing to learn, they reject the knowledge that would enlighten them. She continues, 'modern researchers often miss obvious levels of meaning, because they are insufficiently aware of the society that so closely interpenetrated the stage in Shakespeare's day.'[1] This is simply what I have been urging all along.

I used to wonder how the audience took Shakespeare's constant exposure of the people, showing up their variability and credulity, their foolery. From making fun of them in the early plays to the blistering condemnation in *Julius Caesar* and *Coriolanus*, it is always the same. Now we know that, so far from offending his audiences, which would have been quite unlike him, it would have appealed to them.

When the leading Shakespeare expert in USSR, Professor Alexandr Anikst, sent me his Quatercentenary tribute to Shakespeare, I was taken aback. Shakespeare was made out to be a man of the people, with populist sympathies, etc. The professor must have known better, but I expect that, in those still Stalinist days, if he had told the truth he would have been sacked from the Soviet Writers' Union. But even in democratic societies it is difficult to get truth across, people being what they are.

Whence come the courtship scenes in French between Henry V and Catherine of France? We do not have far to look. Earlier this century an important piece of information was discovered by an amateur researcher, C. W. Wallace – no professor. In the Public Record Office he brought to light a lawsuit which revealed Shakespeare lodging about this time in the French household of the Mountjoys (Montjoie) in Silver Street, just down the road from Cripplegate. German

[1] ibid., ix.

bombs obliterated this little street, but we have a depiction of it in Ralph Agas' map of about 1560. There is the shop, with a pentice in front. I have reproduced it for the reader in *Shakespeare the Man*.

It would have been a shop, for the Mountjoys were 'tire-' or wig-makers. Shakespeare was lodging here about 1600–2, probably before, and performed the betrothal of the Mountjoys' daughter to their apprentice, one Bellot, another French name. Shakespeare is described, in 1612, as 'of Stratford upon Avon, gentleman, of the age of 48 or thereabouts.' Precisely: he was born in 1564. At Madame Montjoie's request he performed the betrothal; so he was evidently on terms of confidence with the lady. Later, I was able to add a nugget of information about her from Forman's papers: she lost two rings and a French crown from her purse as she went along the street.[1] This was in 1597; we learn that she was then thirty, three years younger than her respected lodger, 'Master' Shakespeare.

From *Henry V* to *Henry VIII* is a long jump – to the last play the now famous playwright completed. All commentators have noted how different it is from the other history plays, but none of them realised why, until recently Glynne Wickham, both scholar and pro-ducer, threw light upon it. I have been able to throw a little more.

It is the way it is *because of the political circumstances of the time*, now a matter of history. *Macbeth* had paid tribute to the new King, James I, with his Scottish ancestry, and included a prophetic augury for his line on the throne. *Cymbeline* was to do just this again, as does *Henry VIII*. No wonder that Shakespeare was in favour with James, who doubled the rate of remuneration for performances at Court, and made the leading 'fellows' of the Company Grooms of the Chamber.

James, bent on maintaining peace in Europe, was engaged in a difficult balancing-act: he hoped to marry his son and heir to a Catho-lic Spanish Infanta and his daughter to a German Protestant prince. The subject of Henry VIII was no less ticklish: there was the Reforma-tion, and there was the Divorce of Queen Catherine of Aragon. Neither of these could be well seen in Spanish eyes. Henry himself was an awkward subject: no-one approved his cruelty – it had even

[1] v. *Simon Forman: Sex and Society in Shakespeare's Age*, 97–8.

been attacked by Salisbury recently in the House of Lords. On the other hand, he was the father of the late Queen: nothing could be said against him publicly, though he had wantonly killed her mother.

What an impossible mixture to handle on the stage! Only one writer at the time could be trusted to do it – and that was the Master, about to retire as the Company's full-time dramatist. It is fascinating to watch how he handled this explosive subject.

Negotiations with Spain for an Anglo-Spanish marriage were going forward, and historians know what a special influence the Spanish ambassador, Gondomar, had with James. So – the Divorce of Catherine of Aragon is blamed on Cardinal Wolsey, an unpopular figure with both sides, Catholic as well as Protestant. The rôles of Henry VIII and Anne Boleyn in it are played down – as are their characters: in the play she is hardly more than a lay-figure, while Henry is depicted as rather passive – which was far from the case in historical fact. The finest rôle is given to Catherine of Aragon, Dr Johnson thought perhaps the finest in all the plays. Now *at last* we know why.

At Queen Elizabeth's departure from the scene – so shortly after executing Essex and condemning Southampton – Shakespeare had no word of farewell for her. Now, at her baptism in the play, he pays her a noble tribute which has the accent of farewell, though in the future tense:

> She shall be
> A pattern to all princes living with her,
> And all that shall succeed . . .
> She shall be loved and feared; her own shall bless her;
> Her foes shake like a field of beaten corn.

(Always the countryman's image.) This is followed by a no less enthusiastic tribute to her successor:

> So shall she leave her blessedness to one
> Who, from the sacred ashes of her honour,
> Shall star-like rise, as great in fame as she was . . .

(This was far from the case.)

> His honour and the greatness of his name
> Shall be, and make new nations; he shall flourish
> And, like a mountain cedar, reach his branches
> To all the plains about him . . .

Shakespeare had already used this image of 'the mountain cedar' in

Cymbeline – it comes from the accounts of Virginia in Hakluyt's *Voyages*, of which the playwright was a reader.

James I's plans for keeping peace in Europe came to nothing, but at least 'the new nations' across the Atlantic would come into being. Southampton took a leading part in planting them: Southampton (now Chickahominy) Hundred, Hampton River and Hampton Roads recall him.

6
Light on the Later Plays

I have shown that Shakespeare and Marlowe were closer than people had realised – even than F.P.Wilson in his Clark Lectures at Cambridge, *Marlowe and the Early Shakespeare*. I had been asked to give the first Trevelyan Lectures there, since they were historical; but never the Clark Lectures, since they were literary – out of my 'field', according to the careless cliché.

The publication of Marlowe's *Hero and Leander* in 1598 is reflected in *As You Like It*. The impression it made is still noticeable next year in *Much Ado About Nothing*. A leading character, the much-abused young lady, is named Hero; and Leander's name occurs. Once more it brings home to us that the player-playwright-producer was very much a reading man, if of necessity a quick one, in touch with the best writing coming out at the time.[1] By the same token he had not the time for bumbling about the town, unlike Ben Jonson, let alone for travels abroad, as some have conjectured.

Among personal touches in *Much Ado* is a light-hearted passage about verse-making and rhyming. Some names 'run smoothly in the even road of a blank verse'; Benedick 'can find out no rhyme to "lady" but "baby", an innocent rhyme; for "scorn", "horn", a hard rhyme [probably with a bawdy gesture, since Elizabethan acting was very gestural]; for "school" "fool", a babbling rhyme. Very ominous endings; no, I was not born under a rhyming planet.' Shakespeare

[1] cf my *Shakespeare's Globe*; American edition, *What Shakespeare Read and Thought*.

was: we can see how easily rhyming came to him, a natural poet, unlike the formless anarchy today in the 'verse' promoted by the media. Pope has a line for it:

It is not poetry, but prose run mad.

The transcript from real life of Dogberry and Verges, Constable and Headborough, bears out John Aubrey: 'Ben Jonson and he did gather humours of men daily wherever they came.' The character of Dogberry, Aubrey thought, was picked up from a constable 'at Grendon in Bucks', presumably Long Crendon, along one route between Stratford and London.

We need not doubt the early tradition that *The Merry Wives of Windsor* was written at the command of Elizabeth I, who wished to see 'the fat knight in love', and that it was written in a fortnight – the more swiftly, since it is mostly in prose. We know that the character of Falstaff was bandied about in the Southampton circle, from a letter of his wife to him in Ireland.[1] We have noted Shakespeare's lodging in the French household of the Montjoies at this time. The play makes fun of Dr Caius, a French physician and his comic accent – he makes fritters of English. And where did the author get the rather rare French word 'oeuillades' from?

He had had to change the name intended, 'Oldcastle', to Falstaff, owing to the objection of Lord Cobham. His family name was Brooke, so now Shakespeare had also to change that name, by which Ford was to have disguised himself, to Broome. The play was written for the occasion of a feast of the Order of the Garter. Cobham was made a Knight of the Garter in 1599, and entertained the Queen in Blackfriars in 1600. Briefly his father had been Lord Chamberlain for six months in 1596–7, upon whose death the second Lord Hunsdon succeeded to the post.

There was nothing new to add about *Twelfth Night* (1601), though it had an early interest for me: as a schoolboy I had to play the part of Malvolio.

We note again how keenly Shakespeare was aware of everything going on. 'The new map with the augmentation to the Indies' is

[1] q. in my *Shakespeare's Southampton*, 144.

Mollineux's map of the world on a new projection, which had appeared in 1599. 'You are now sailed into the North ... where you will hang like an icicle on a Dutchman's beard.' This referred to the Dutchman Barentz's recent Arctic voyage of 1596–7. A couple of references to the Sophy (or Shah) of Persia relate to the Shirley brothers' journey, the account of which appeared in 1600.

Orsino, Duke of Bracchiano, paid a visit to the Queen in January, 1601. Shakespeare picked up the name – magpie that he was – for his Duke. That is all that we can say firmly about it, though Hotson erected a whole volume of conjectures upon it. More appealing is the fact that Thomas Morley set the music for the song, 'It was a lover and his lass', and perhaps also for 'O mistress mine'. He lived too in Bishopsgate – nice to think that the poet so devoted to music may have known him. A number of musical compositions were dedicated to Lord Chamberlain Hunsdon, so perhaps he was able to appreciate Emilia's musical as well as her other attractions.

More important to my mind is *Troilus and Cressida* of about 1602, a most exciting play intellectually and thereby least popular. I had seen a fine modern production of it, dressed in the uniforms of the 1914–18 war, during the cynical disillusioned post-war period, for which the play had its message. The pivotal part of Ulysses was taken by my friend Robert Speaight who well understood it, for, a good Shakespearean, he wrote a biography illuminating from the actor's point of view.

A curious Preface described the play as 'never staled by the stage, never clapper-clawed with the palms of the vulgar', so it would seem to have been written for private production. It praised 'especially this author's comedies, that are so framed to the life that they serve for the most common commentaries of all the actions of our lives.' Then follows a boost of the author: 'when he is gone and his comedies out of sale, you will scramble for them'. Evidently an early example of a publisher's blurb, but so good a text must have come from within the Company.

A personal note appears in the Prologue. Something had occurred between touchy Ben Jonson and his kindly disposed senior. William had recruited him to the Company with his *Everyman in his Humour* in 1598, and had acted in his *Everyman out of his Humour* next year. The irreverent junior had a jest at Shakespeare's taking to a coat of arms, *Non sans droit*, not without right. (Wasn't that in character, consistent with all that we have said about him?) Ben suggested for crest, 'Not without mustard', and for coat 'a hog's cheek and puddings'.

Shortly there occurred the theatre-warfare between the men's companies and the boys', referred to in *Hamlet*. Ben took umbrage – not apparently with William, difficult to quarrel with – but he left the Chamberlain's Men for the Boys, who specialised in satire. For his *Poetaster* he provided a Prologue, who came in armed to launch self-confident defiance at his detractors. Now Shakespeare provides

> A Prologue armed, but not in confidence
> Of author's pen, or actor's voice, but suited
> In like conditions as our argument.

Once more it confirms our view of him. Everything is consistent about him. As he had urged in *Hamlet*, all must be subordinated to the artistic demands of the play, its 'argument'. He wrote not only from direct inspiration, 'the child of nature', but as a conscious artist with his own aesthetic.

This play has all the atmosphere of the time in it – above all disenchantment with the long war, and to the unwarlike playwright its pointlessness. There is the embittered factionalism of the last years of the reign, the breaking apart of the earlier patriotic unity. There is the disillusionment now with the chivalrous figure upon whom so many hopes had been placed:

> Things small as nothing, for request's sake only,
> He makes important.

That had been his regular way with the Queen, who found it intolerable. Now –

> what the declined is
> He shall as soon read in the eyes of others
> As feel in his own fall. For men, like butterflies,
> Show not their mealy wings but to the summer . . .

The experience of love for a faithless woman, with its disenchantment, is a main theme of this private play. More pressing are the lessons it enforces about society, the absolute necessity of order and obedience if things were not to break down into anarchy. Further than that, the necessity of social differentiation according to function, the proper observance of degree and difference, of quality, of 'authentic place'.

> The general's disdained
> By him one step below, he by the next,
> That next by him beneath. So every step
> Exampled by the first pace that is sick
> Of his superior, grows to an envious fever
> Of pale and bloodless emulation.

That might well have been written of our sick society of the Sixties, when everything went wrong and anarchy threatened. An egalitarian society releases envy and emulation at every level. We have had comparable anarchy in the arts: the new brutalism in architecture, with no sense of order or proportion; a similar lack of order, or even of sense, in the verse patronised by the media – and a censorship exercised against those who did not conform to it; anarchy in the visual arts by those who couldn't draw, any more than the 'poets' could rhyme or scan. Stephen Spender has asked the question whether the poets of the past would recognise the 'verse' of today as poetry at all. The novel, appropriately for such a society, specialised in violence, murder, rape, racial miscegenation; mugging, thugging, drugging. An excellent traditional novelist, Barbara Pym, could not even get her novels published during those years. Though that was more disgraceful, I found something of that paralleled in the attitude to my own work: both symptomatic of a squalid society.

There are signs that this state of things is now being recognised for what it is. My recognition of it while it was at its height was not welcome, any more than my depiction of Shakespeare as a prime exponent of social order. What he thought of the masses is obvious throughout his work: their sheer destructiveness when out of the bonds of discipline, left to their own sweet will. In *2 Henry VI* we have the impulse of the commons to destroy: 'Now go, some, and pull down the Savoy; others to the Inns of Court. Down with them all!' In the Peasants' Revolt of 1381 the mob had destroyed John of Gaunt's palace of the Savoy, with its jewels, tapestries, books, illuminated manuscripts. In *Julius Caesar*, 1599, we have the mob crying out: 'Burn! Fire! Kill! . . . Go fetch fire. Pluck down benches. Pluck down forms, windows, anything.' The play shows up their

credulity, the ineffectiveness of the doctrinaire Brutus' appeal to reason, while Mark Antony can twist the idiots round his finger by
appealing to their emotions, their inveterate unreason.

The treatment of Shakespeare's view of politics and society – as
such a *responsible* one – was a prime feature of my book. This aspect
of his work had been hitherto disregarded by literary folk who did
not understand it, and again no notice was taken of this particular
contribution to the understanding of Shakespeare. Nor do I think
that the exposure of what the masses really are is ever welcome to
idealogues who prefer their illusions about them.

We come to *All's Well that Ends Well*, 1602–3: here I have much
that is new to offer. The background was readily recognisable. The
scene was laid in France, the King a leading character, French names
of lords, etc. No-one had noticed that the play was written about
the time that the author was lodging in the French household of
the Montjoies. The sickness of the King sets the action going. During
this queasy time Elizabeth I was visibly moving towards her end.
Sickness and plague were all around – 1603 was a year of exceptionally heavy 'visitation', as Elizabethans called it. The King has been
given up by the doctors of the 'congregated College': that was as
near as one dared to refer to the Royal College of Physicians, who
persecuted empirics like 'Dr' Forman. The King cannot 'prostitute
our past-cure malady to empirics'.

The action concerns a spoiled young Count who refuses to marry
the girl who heals the King but is socially beneath the Count, filled
with aristocratic pride. His mother, the Countess, favours the marriage, and is fearful of his incurring the disfavour of the King by
his refusal. Rather than consummate the marriage the adolescent
Count flounces off to Italy to the wars, where he performs bravely
enough.

Where have we met this situation before?

It is precisely the situation of Southampton in regard to marriage,
with something of the characteristics and even of the characters
recognisable. He had for years refused marriage, as we have seen;
until almost the term of Elizabeth Vernon's pregnancy in 1598 he
had delayed marrying her, flouncing off to France. Yet in Ireland
next year he had performed gallantly enough in this field. He had

never won the Queen's favour. When he was condemned to death with Essex, his mother made this, his despair of ever winning the royal favour, her plea for mercy.

Bernard Shaw thought the character of the Count's mother the most charming portrait of a woman in the Plays. We recognise her in the tribute to her in the Sonnets:

> Thou art thy mother's glass, and she in thee
> Calls back the lovely April of her prime.

It is likely enough that she welcomed her son's poet helping in the campaign they all advanced – mother, grandfather, his guardian Lord Burghley – to get him safely married.

In the play the most idiosyncratic character is the braggadocio captain Parolles: a realistic transcript, if a caricature, from the life of the time. The wars had been going on long enough for such a type to be around and about. Southampton had such a one with him in Ireland. We learn from the State Papers that, when Southampton was General of Horse there (as Count Bertram was made in the play), he had one Captain Piers Edmonds as his companion. 'He ate and drank at his table, and lay in his tent. The Earl of Southampton would cull and hug him in his arms and play wantonly with him.' I do not wish to enter the never-never land of conjecture: I should simply like to know more about this Captain, on familiar terms in the circle – Essex would take him in his coach with him. I can find only that he was a cockney, born in the Strand.

So far I have come across only one who even saw the clear transcript this play offers from its author's experience. That was an unknown young American scholar, writing (I recall) in the *Modern Language Review*, when the grandees had never noticed it. Yet a conventional editor of the play could comment generally on 'the creative interplay between author and environment, the fact that the feelings of the author are a creative part of the climate of opinion in which he lives'.[1] Notice the *cliché* 'climate of opinion': it is not other people's *opinion* that inspired Shakespeare but the facts and events, the people and characters, he experienced and observed.

This editor did notice that 'Shakespeare had some knowledge of French, and the atmosphere of the play is decidedly French. The names ... seem to indicate a mind at work strongly imbued with

---

[1] *All's Well that Ends Well*, *The Arden Shakespeare*, ed. G.K.Hunter, liii.

a consciousness of French meanings.'[1] How typical – missing the significance that the writer was at the time an intimate of the French household in Silver Street!

James I succeeded Elizabeth in 1603: a contrast in every way, except that both were well-educated and intelligent, and both loved the theatre – as Puritans did not. For one thing, James was homosexual; Elizabeth, though something of a feminist, was not Lesbian. But she was a great actress, always playing to the gallery, showing off to the mob (like her mother, she had a streak of popular vulgarity). James, however, could not abide crowds. A timorous man – and with reason from the Scottish background of assassination – he made it clear on coming to England that he did not wish people pressing in upon him.

So we find immediately in *Measure for Measure*, 1604, the point put tactfully as ever:

> I love the people

(did he?)

> But do not like to stage me to their eyes.

(note the word 'stage' here: Elizabeth I had always been on the stage, all too visible.)

> Though it do well, I do not relish well
> Their loud applause ...

Then, with a flash-back to Essex:

> Nor do I think the man of safe discretion
> That does affect it.

The playwright makes the point:

> The general [populace], subject to a well-wished king,
> Quit their own part, and in obsequious fondness
> Crowd to his presence, where their untaught love
> Must needs appear offence.

The unpopular, undemocratic point could not be put more tactfully.

[1] ibid., xxv.

There was nothing new to say about *Othello*, 1604; but I emphasised that Othello was a Moor, i.e. he was dark, as North Africans are, but not a black. Nevertheless, just as *The Merchant of Venice* turned on the Jewish issue, now *Othello* turned on the racialist, dark skin against white. These issues are still deplorably alive: they witness, if nothing else, to the author's universality.

The theme of witchcraft, spells and 'medicines bought of mounte-banks' comes in; Othello's fatal handkerchief had been 'dyed in mummy', a concoction made from mummies or corpses (which For-man dealt in, by the way). The plague of 1603 is still in the back-ground, the raven 'o'er the infected house boding to all'.

November 1605 was signalised by the Gunpowder Plot. A 'knot' – the contemporary word for it – of crazy young Catholics planned to blow up King, Lords and Commons at the opening of Parliament, from a cellar beneath stacked with gunpowder. The affair made an immense sensation. One effect was that it ended any prospect of further toleration for Catholics. Another was a surge of popular feel-ing for the new royal house, James I and his family thus threatened.

In the way with which we are now familiar the popular dramatist turned this to account with *Macbeth*, 1606. He took a suitably dra-matic subject from Scottish history in Holinshed, the murder of king Duncan and his supersession by Macbeth. We have the first of his tactful tributes to James I in the character of Banquo, putative ances-tor of the Stuarts:

> And to that dauntless temper of his mind
> He hath a wisdom that doth guide his valour
> To act in safety . . .

'Dauntless', 'valour'! – James was a timid soul, but he was not wanting in sense, and knew how to 'act in safety'. The play features the pro-phecy that Banquo should be 'father to a line of kings'. A dumb-show follows with the line of eight kings.

> What will the line stretch out to the crack of doom? . . .

> And yet the eighth appears, who bears a glass
> Which shows me many more, and some
> That two-fold balls and treble sceptres carry, I see.

This eighth was James; the 'two-fold balls' are the orbs of England and Scotland, the third sceptre represents the claim to France which still appeared in the royal title. As for the line carrying on to 'the crack of doom', the prophecy has not done badly; for the line descending from James I is still with us.

With his Scotch Calvinist background he had some doubt, on coming to England, about performing the traditional right of touching for the 'king's evil'. This was the sacrosanct rite performed by European kings, such sanctified persons as Charles II and Louis XIV, in healing by their touch persons suffering from scrofula and such horrors. The rite was to continue in England so long as the Stuarts did – Dr Johnson, as a boy, was 'touched' by Queen Anne. (It did him no good, but confirmed his Jacobite feelings.)

Macbeth has a long passage devoted to this nonsense – a matter of anthropological rather than medical interest.

> At his touch
> Such sanctity hath heaven given his hand
> They presently amend . . .
> A most miraculous work in this good king,
> Which often since my here-remain in England
> I have seen him do. How he solicits heaven
> Himself best knows. But strangely-visited people,
> All swollen and ulcerous, pitiful to the eye,
> The mere despair of surgery, he cures;
> Hanging a golden stamp about their necks,
> Put on with holy prayers . . .
>
> To the succeeding royalty he leaves
> The healing benediction. With this strange virtue
> He hath a heavenly gift of prophecy,
> And sundry blessings hang about his throne
> That speak him full of grace.

This kind of thing was not displeasing to the monarch, and it was a fair return for his taking Shakespeare's Company under his patronage as the King's Men. During the plague of 1603 the Court took refuge in the country at Wilton, where both Southampton and the younger Pembroke were in attendance, and Shakespeare's Company performed. Here indeed is matter for conjecture, such memories were present in the company. But we refrain from conjecture . . . That *Love's Labour's Lost* had a personal association for Southampton is indicated by his having it revived for performance, though an old play, when James visited Southampton House in 1605.

Echoes of Gunpowder Plot itself are present in *Macbeth*. Henry Garnet, Provincial of the Jesuits, had lived quietly in England for years. Now he had learned of the existence of a plot by these young desperadoes, but under the seal of confession he had not thought proper to give warning. Even the Catholic Northampton reproached him with this at his examination. Then the Jesuit doctrine of equivocation came up: one need not tell the truth when under pressure, one might equivocate. This made a bad popular impression: it was thought somehow un-English, and indeed it was specially favoured by the Jesuits abroad. Hence in the play an equivocator is one 'that could swear in both scales against either scale, who committed treason enough for God's sake, yet could not equivocate to heaven'.

Shakespeare was never one for going against popular sentiment, as we saw years before with his reference to the Jesuits in the Sonnets:

> the fools of time
> Which die for goodness who have lived for crime.

With the accession of James, Southampton had the sense at last to turn his coat and conform. Thereupon he was taken into favour; some people expected that he might become a groom of the bedchamber. But he was rather old for that, and at last happily married; moreover, he was not James's 'type', young Robert Carr was, and the job pre-empted.

Nothing new to be said of *King Lear*, except to point out that the Company visited Dover in August 1606, the summer before the play was written. Hence the description of 'Shakespeare's Cliff' there. Conservative traditionalist as I am, I have shown how authentic the early traditions are. Deer-stealing at Stratford, for example: hunting the deer is there in all the early work, plays and poems. Nothing discreditable in it – just the thing that bright young sparks did engage in. Simon Forman tells us of his young Oxford clerics poaching the Queen's deer up at Shotover.

With the character of Cleopatra (*Antony and Cleopatra*, 1607) we come to something personally significant. The play is a celebration of a world-famous love; yet there is something curiously ambivalent about it, something nostalgic, not without a suggestion of disillusion – no illusion anyway. The personality of Cleopatra is like no other woman in the plays. She is above all temperamental, contrarious, undependable. She knows that that is the way to hold her man: keep him on tenterhooks. When her waiting woman thinks that she should 'give him way, cross him in nothing', Cleopatra knows instinctively that the opposite is the right line:

> Thou teachest like a fool: the way to lose him.

Where have we met this before? – In Rosaline in *Love's Labour's Lost*:

> How I would make him fawn, and beg, and seek . . .
> And shape his service wholly to my hests . . .
> So planet-like would I o'er-sway his state,
> That he should be my fool, and I his fate.

Cleopatra has this in common with Rosaline – and all recognise that Rosaline was Shakespeare's Dark Lady.

The essential quality of Cleopatra was that she was alien to Rome, her very foreignness. Agatha Christie, with her instinct for detection, was convinced that in creating this unique character Shakespeare was *remembering*, depicting someone he had known. Nor does Antony spare her, when she betrays him: 'triple-turned whore', etc, any more than the woman in the Sonnets is spared after her betrayal of Shakespeare. We may conclude equably that the play, like the Sonnets, displays both sides of heterosexual love.

Even in this erotic play distaste for the people has expression:

> mechanic slaves
> With greasy aprons, rules and hammers shall
> Uplift us to the view. In their thick breaths,
> Rank of gross diet, shall we be enclouded,
> And forced to drink their vapour.

We find a similar description of them in the next play, *Coriolanus*, 1608:

> the kitchen malkin pins
> Her richest lockram 'bout her reechy neck,
> Clambering the walls to eye him. Stalls, bulks, windows
> Are smothered up, leads filled, and ridges horsed
> With variable complexions . . .

Not much sympathy for the under-privileged there! Indeed, he never had any – he had had too much of a struggle himself to sentimentalise about those of whom there are far too many. Everywhere, and all through history, wherever there is subsistence humans will breed without control, like other animals.

Two facts emerge about the new play. First, in regard to Style. Ben Jonson was critical of his senior for being insufficiently classical. This objection runs through French eighteenth-century criticism, notably with Voltaire. It is true that neither the classical ideal nor satire was in keeping with Shakespeare's spirit. Yet this perfect Johannes Factotum could write a classical play if he wished – witness *Julius Caesar* and *Coriolanus*. Both these plays have classical lines, rather *raide*: no comic sub-plot, no mixture of tragedy with comedy which is characteristic of him and yields such rich effects. Neither of these Roman plays is luxuriant: they are not exactly bleak, but they make few concessions to sentiment or sympathy from their uncompromising Roman standard.

The theme of this play is the modern one of Class Conflict, so universal is this writer's appeal that he reaches forward to today in this, as in other respects. For all the large cast that the play requires, its two essential protagonists are Coriolanus and the People.

In May 1607 there were agrarian disturbances in the Midlands, especially in Warwickshire, where Shakespeare was now a land-owner. He had been able, with his profits from the theatre, to pur-chase 107 acres of the best land in Old Stratford (think what it would be worth today!). A bigger buy was one-half of all the tithes in and around Stratford, Bishopton, Welcombe, etc. That was a large invest-ment, more than enough to maintain the status of an independent gentleman.

Most of the complaints arose from enclosure, and we know from independent evidence that in this matter he was involved. The State Papers tell us that there was a great outcry about 'dearth', the dearness and scarcity of corn. The peasantry complained that some of the well-to-do were holding back stores from the market for higher prices. Actually the provident gentleman of New Place had a considerable store of malt in the big house. (Why not? It is the provident, not the wasteful or meek, who inherit the earth.)

Here is the subject of the first scene. The citizens' cry is 'What authority surfeits on would relieve us ... They ne'er cared for us yet, and their store-houses crammed with grain – make edicts for usury to support usurers. And provide more statutes daily to chain up and restrain the poor.' This refers to the Poor Law statutes of 1598 and 1601 which, however unpopular, did provide something towards the problem of people who proliferate beyond the means of subsistence.

The wisdom of the people regards Coriolanus as their chief enemy, since he is the outstanding man in the state, who in fact has saved it. 'Let us kill him, and we'll have corn at our own price.' The patrician, who represents the point of view of government – and William Shakespeare's – tries to explain to them that the dearth is nobody's fault, it comes from natural causes (just like 'curing' unemployment, when there are simply too many people).

The action of the play turns on the mistake the soldierly Coriolanus makes in submitting himself for election to office, to the people for whom he has nothing but contempt. He lets them see this, when a *politician* would have talked the humbug they like to hear. Remember that 'politician' is always a pejorative term with Shakespeare; and in the play we have two plausible 'tribunes of the people', who twist the good citizens round their fingers and feed their hatred for the great man who has saved Rome. (It is like Leftists of the *Tribune* attacking Churchill.) They end up, 'To the Rock, to the Rock with him!' He is driven into exile: 'The people's enemy is gone, is gone.' 'They all shout and throw up their caps' is the stage direction. They cry: 'Our enemy is banished, he is gone. Hoo-oo!'

So much for the electorate. We must be fair: not always do they get it wrong, sometimes they even get it right. But we see how thoroughly this observer from the stage and behind the scenes understood politics, and how relevant this work was to political facts and conditions always. An eminent American historian, himself a liberal democrat, once remarked to me that the instinct of American democracy is 'to lop the tallest'.

Ironically, the intellectuals lend themselves to this process – ironically, for their supposed claim is to be more intelligent. In his *Armageddon* Gore Vidal has an attack on President Reagan as leader of a crusade against Soviet Russia: it shows up the intellectual's judgment when in fact President Reagan took the completely opposite line. Similarly George Orwell made a fortune with his *1984*, elaborating how much worse, even more Stalinist, Soviet Russia would become by then. In fact, the 1980s witness Russia attempting to re-enter Western civilisation.

Why are intellectuals so silly? They should study Shakespeare: he was not an 'intellectual', like Marlowe or Ben Jonson. They would not have thought of him as one. The joke is that in fact he was cleverer than they were.

Nor is his observation simply of the surface of things, his comments negative: he penetrates to the heart of the matter – as in *Troilus and Cressida*:

> There is a mystery, in whom relation
> Durst never meddle, in the soul of state –

this is what Burke and Dr Johnson understood, as liberal rationalists never do –

> Which hath an operation more divine
> Than breath or pen can give expressure to.

This is also true: the heart of the matter *is* difficult to define, and ordinary people can never be expected to understand it. – As that professed democrat, Franklin Roosevelt, *said*, but never out loud: 'The public never understands.'

Shakespeare well understood the consequences,

> where gentry, title, wisdom,
> Cannot conclude but by the yea and no
> Of general ignorance.

The effect is to

> bereave the state
> Of that integrity which should become it –
> Not having the power to do the good it would
> For the ill which doth control it.

Throughout the post-war period one could observe with disgust a state of society which

> must omit
> Real necessities . . .
> Purpose so barred, it follows,
> Nothing is done to purpose.

To call attention to it, point out the dangers, was to be thought 'eccentric':

> manhood is called foolery when it stands
> Against a falling fabric.

One still does not know whether the rescue-operation so hopefully undertaken in the 1980s is not too late, nor whether it will last.

People do not like to be told home-truths. Shakespeare said out loud what he thought. In the 1930s when *Coriolanus* was put on in Paris there were riots – so little did democracy like its salutary message.

Timon of Athens, 1608–9, follows *Coriolanus* and has much in common with it, cynical in its depiction of foolery on all sides – as if Swift were to write a play. Shakespeare's attitude towards the people had hardened since the early days, when he saw at least the comic side of them. There is nothing comic in his portrayal of them in *Troilus and Cressida*, *Coriolanus*, and *Timon*. E.K.Chambers, a pre-1914 Liberal, was appalled. We have been through such horrors since his happy Victorian days that we take them for granted. Chambers wrote of these plays: 'in each alike we find the same readiness of bitter criticism, the same remorseless analysis, probing and dissecting, as with a cruel scalpel, the intimate weaknesses and basenesses of mankind. In each, ideals are shattered, heroes are discrowned and stripped of their heroism.' He concludes innocently, 'it is with difficulty that our sympathies, so essential to the sense of tragedy, are retained'.

That reveals him as incapable of appreciating Shakespeare's universality, the horrors as well as the delights, the depths of human nature along with the heights. Living in our appalling time, with our experience, we appreciate better how right he was.

Timon was never finished. Here I had two pertinent questions to ask. Had the writer reached the term of disillusion? Even the sober Chambers was willing to risk a biographical conjecture at this point. What we can say is that this bitterness was not in keeping with his inner nature, confirmed as it is by John Aubrey. Secondly, the unfinished state of the play reveals how he wrote his plays. – As a theatre-man would – not like a modern writer starting at the beginning and going straight on: he wrote the scenes as he *saw* them. Thus the beginning and the end have completed scenes; the middle is a rough draft, first thoughts jotted down sometimes in prose, sometimes in blank verse or rhymed couplets, just as it came.

A further reflection is how revealing the play was of the new Jacobean age – the opulence, the ostentatious extravagance, the banquets and the bankruptcies. Again I found the art-patter of the painter, the mutual flattery of painter and poet, the insincerity and humbug true enough to such exchanges at all times. Already Virginia was in mind. Jamestown had been started in 1607. Instead of ploughing and planting the rag-tag-and-bobtail took to digging for gold: there was a perfect craze for gold, and shortly the fools were starving. The report came back: 'no talk, no hope, no work but to dig gold, wash gold, refine gold, load gold'. There wasn't any, and shortly they were digging for roots for sustenance, like Timon on the seashore. But he found gold:

> Gold! Yellow, glittering precious gold!
>   . . . Thus much of this will make
> Black white, foul fair, wrong right,
> Base noble, old young, coward valiant . . .
>   place thieves
> And give them title, knee, and approbation
> With senators on the bench.

In the Jacobean age money talked as never before. Peerages were bought, as they were not under Elizabeth I; knighthoods proliferated, a new order of baronets created to satisfy aspirants; all James's young men reached the senators' bench, James Hay, Robert Carr, George Villiers. This last, handsomest of men, not only became a duke, but all his grasping family were ennobled and richly endowed from the public funds.

What does one do when sick with disillusion? One turns from a world gone sour to the world of romance, to poetry and the inner life of the imagination, in a sense one comes home again.

It is maddening that we have such a poor 'reported' text of the first two Acts of *Pericles*, 1608; for it was Shakespeare's first experiment in a new vein of romance, and was a noted success. In this year the Burbages took back the little Blackfriars theatre they owned, which had been hitherto leased to the Boys' Companies. The dramatist, their leading 'Fellow', became part-owner. Here was a more

sophisticated, upper-class audience to cater for – indoor, winter performances, lights, music, better stage effects. This called for a new
accent, more fairy-tale and music, less blood-and-thunder; henceforth the all-providing playwright of the Company would be writing
for both audiences, himself freer to remain more in the country.

Circumstances were responsible for the problem the text of *Pericles*
presents.[1] Plague was to the fore again: there was a hiatus in the
theatres, closed for a year and a half, as also in publishing. A text
was announced but, alas, not printed: what we have of the first
two Acts is a mangled mass from, apparently, two unintelligent
reporters.

I do not enter into these highly specialised textual discussions,
dominated by acute differences of opinion about who printed what,
which compositor, A, B, or C. What interests me more is something
others have not noticed, more relevant to Shakespeare than compositors after all. As usual the subject may have been suggested by
a book that came out the year before, by Lawrence Twine, in 1607.
But to make a play the playwright thought up something new. It
would have a remote, archaic flavouring; he would provide a Chorus,
who would have an important part and speak in antique rhymed
octosyllabic couplets.

Very appropriately, for John Gower was made the Chorus, and
his was the version of the story used, from his best-known poem,
Confessio Amantis. What I noticed was that Gower's tomb dominated
the church of St Saviour's, Southwark, along Bankside from the
Globe. The church is now Southwark Cathedral, and the tomb has
been moved to a less conspicuous position. But you can still go and
see it, the old poet, a contemporary of Chaucer, resting there with
his books, one of which is his *Confessio Amantis*. Shakespeare was
one who noticed such things, not only 'bare ruined choirs' as he
went about the country, but especially monuments and tombs – to
which references are scattered all through his works.

Those two areas meant something special to him: Blackfriars from
beginning to end, and Southwark across the river from the time that
the Globe was set up there. St Saviour's was the church of the Bankside
vicinity, and at this very time, the last day in the year 1607, Shakespeare's young brother Edmund, another actor, had been buried

[1] A good account of all this is by Philip Edwards, 'An Approach to the Problem
of *Pericles*', *Shakespeare Survey*, vol. 5, 26 foll.

there. When you go to Southwark Cathedral, look for his stone. The young fellow, only twenty-seven, was buried that cold Christmas when the Thames froze over, 'with a forenoon knell of the great bell'.[1] Quite a considerable fee for that attention was paid – by whom? Do we need to conjecture?

The success of *Pericles* is further witnessed by George Wilkins' cashing in on it with a tale, *The Painful Adventures of Pericles, Prince of Tyre*. He plagiarised from the play, thus enabling editors to fill in some bits of a ruined text. Roger Prior has thrown a flood of light – from historical research, not conjecture – upon this literary-minded inn-keeper, whose inn was patronised by theatre-folk.[2] Among his lodgers were the young Bellot couple, from the Montjoie household, whom 'Master Shakespeare' had betrothed.

The more one researches into the facts the more they connect up and become real and alive. One does not need superfluous conjectures.

For *Cymbeline*, 1609, I had also a new contribution to make. Why are the Romans made to land at Milford Haven of all out-of-the-way places? Historically, the Romans never did. Why does so much of the action take place there? My friend Douglas Jay, a good Shakespearean, wondered why and asked me. It had not occurred to any 'expert' to wonder why; and no Eng. Lit. person to whom I put the question could ever answer it, yet a young historian at All Souls spotted the answer at once. It was because this was where James I's great-great-grandfather, Henry VII, had landed in 1485 before Bosworth Field, through whom came James's claim to the English throne. Once more the play is a tribute to the generous patron of the King's Men. The shadow of the new British King stands behind that of the old British King; his two sons stand for James's two sons, Prince Henry and Prince Charles, and the only daughter, Imogen, for James's only daughter, Elizabeth.

The play, like *Macbeth* and *Henry VIII*, has yet another tribute to the Royal family in the form of a prophecy:

> The lofty cedar, royal Cymbeline,
> Personates thee; and thy lopped branches point

[1] Mark Eccles, *Shakespeare in Warwickshire*, 107.
[2] Roger Prior, 'The Life of George Wilkins', *Shakespeare Survey*, vol. 25, 137 foll.; and 'George Wilkins and the Young Heir', *Shakespeare Survey*, vol. 29, 33 foll.

Thy two sons forth . . .
                                    are now revived,
To the majestic cedar joined: whose issue
Promises Britain peace and plenty.

England, now joined with Scotland, had become Britain – James was
naturally keener on that name. A rather absurd pun shadows forth

The piece of tender air, thy virtuous daughter.

This was Elizabeth, ancestress through her marriage to the German
Prince Palatine of the present Royal family. In the celebrations for
her marriage in 1613 the plays of the favourite dramatist were to
occupy one-half of the whole repertory.

There is also a characteristically indirect reference to Richard Field
as Richard du Champ. Shakespeare's Stratford fellow townsman
meant more to him than we have knowledge of, since he printed
the poet's two long poems. Shakespeare was much in and out of
Blackfriars over the years. The letter that sparked off *The Tempest*
came to hand in Blackfriars, and before the end he equipped himself
with a lodging there in one-half of the gatehouse into the precinct.

The Winter's Tale, of 1610–11, takes us back to those earlier associations. For one thing the story comes from Robert Greene's early
romance, *Pandosto*. Notice again what brought it back to mind:
it had recently been republished, in 1607. The countryside is in the
background, and a Cotswold sheep-shearing feast is brought directly
on the stage: shepherds and country folk, ballad-singing, thieving
pedlar and all.

When Simon Forman saw the play at the Globe in May 1611 he
was naturally much interested in the part played by oracle in it, also
by the thieving pedlar and 'how he feigned him sick and to have
been robbed; how he cozened the poor man of all his money; how
he changed apparel with the king of Bohemia's son'. This was much
to Simon's tastes; he ends up like himself, with a warning: 'beware
of trusting feigned beggars or fawning fellows'.[1]

It is well known what, in events at the time, suggested *The Tempest*,
1611: the wreck of the colonists' flagship going to Virginia in 1609,

---

[1] cf. *Simon Forman: Sex and Society in Shakespeare's Age*, 306–7

in a tornado which drove the ship on the coast of Bermuda, where she foundered and broke up. The account of it came back to Black-friars, where the alert dramatist made use of it all down to precise detail. We have not only the enchanted isle, which was thought at the time to be haunted, something of the events on the island – an attempted mutiny – down to the 'St Elmo's fire' running down the rigging, a feature of such equatorial storms. It is all there – the prodigy of a wreck with not a life lost.

What interested me in particular was the way things connect up. Shakespeare was interested in the Voyages to America from his read-ing in Hakluyt. Southampton had all along been interested in Virginia and ended up as Treasurer of the Virginia Company. Now his former household retainer, Florio, had translated Montaigne (appropriately, for both were half-Jewish). Shakespeare was reading his former col-league's book, for he answers back Montaigne's illusions about primi-tive society and the beauty of communist arrangements therein:

> All things in common Nature should produce
> Without sweat or endeavour: treason, felony,
> Sword, pike, knife, gun, or need of any engine,
> Would I not have.

No magistrature or judiciary – certainly no capital punishment or death penalty: 'my innocent people' would not need such things. No private property, no trade, no need to work; 'no occupation', 'all men idle' – Nature would be sufficient and bring forth harvests, 'all abundance'.

It did not need the deaths of millions, in the communisation of agriculture in Soviet Russia, to tell William Shakespeare what non-sense this was. When someone asks,

> No marrying 'mong his subjects?

The answer comes:

> None man, all idle: whores and knaves.

Here is a peculiarity about William Shakespeare: *he never seems to have thought any nonsense at all*. His feet were firmly on the ground; for all his towering imagination he had an indefeasible fund of common sense. His was not the twilight ethicality of do-gooders and liberal illusionists about human nature. He was a practical man; he made money. Why is it that, when it comes to actual thinking, so many men of genius think nonsense? Tolstoy, for instance, thought that neither Shakespeare nor Beethoven was any good; moreover, a lot of what he thought about Christianity and property, giving away all one's goods and making a nuisance of oneself, passive resistance, etc, was illusory, contrary to the facts of human nature.

Much of what Milton or Shelley thought about politics was in contradiction with these. A lot of Bernard Shaw's or H.G.Wells's thinking was just silly; Yeats's stuff about spiritualism and Rosicrucianism and fairies mere baloney. Even Eliot's declaration for Anglo-Catholicism and a censureship exercised by Lambeth Palace was absurd; while Ezra Pound, less of a genius, was half-cracked. We already know what to think of Bertrand Russell and Sartre's thinking, while Brecht's deliberate subscription to Stalinism was simply evil.

We need not question the genius of these people, it is when it comes to *thinking* that they are so apt to think nonsense. I do not fully understand why this should be so. All that is relevant here is that William Shakespeare should have thought none at all.

I have never been much interested in what is called the 'Shakespeare Apocrypha': usually ludicrous suggestions of plays quite out of character and quality for him. Nor for that matter in conjectures about him and his work, by people who should sit down and learn about it, when they do not qualify even to hold an opinion. And so I had not gone into the question of *The Two Noble Kinsmen*, to see how much of it was Shakespeare's, until an unknown, but intelligent, correspondent drew my attention to the close similarity of theme with *The Two Gentlemen of Verona,* which I had shown to be autobiographical. Unlike the Shakespeare Trade Union beyond learning anything, he had taken the point. The theme is again the rivalry of two sworn friends for the love of the same woman.

The story in this case comes from another source, Chaucer's 'Knight's Tale'. The names of the Duke of Athens and his lady Hippolyta recur, but the later play adheres to Chaucer's story, with the rivalry of the young men for Emelye. In this late play the form of the name is Emilia (that loaded name!). Belonging to 1613, it was published in 1634 as by 'Mr John Fletcher and Mr William Shakespeare.' Note the respectfulness of the address 'Mr' (i.e. Master):

Fletcher was the son of a bishop and succeeded Mr Shakespeare as dramatist-in-chief to the King's Men. Evidently the play was regarded as more his than the old master's.

There is considerable agreement as to their respective parts, but I do not arrive at it via computers' dull metrical tests, feminine endings, etc, though I agree that run-on lines are typical of late Shakespeare. I am more interested in unmistakable associations of thought and characteristics at once recognisable.

Most of Act I is regarded as Shakespeare's. We soon encounter a thought that is so regular with him that I call it the 'Shakespeare Paradox':

> where every evil
> Hath a good colour; where every seeming good's
> A certain evil; where not to be even jump
> As they are . . .

All through this actor's writing there is this consciousness of the dichotomy between 'seeming' and 'being'. This odd use of the word 'jump' is frequent with him. 'I will not jump with common spirits.' 'Both our inventions meet and jump in one.' 'Till each circumstance of place, time, fortune, do cohere and jump', etc. The thought itself bears the signature of the author, as in *Henry V*:

> There is some soul of goodness in things evil
> Would men observingly distil it out.

At the end of *The Two Noble Kinsmen* we find the Paradox again, in different words:

> That we should things desire which do cost us
> The loss of our desire! . . .

We find the same sceptical thought, so true to his temperament, in *Antony and Cleopatra*:

> We, ignorant of ourselves,
> Beg often our own harms, which the wise powers
> Deny us for our good: so we find profit
> By losing of our prayers.

Turn to the concluding lines of *The Two Noble Kinsmen*:

> O you heavenly Charmers,
> What things you make of us! For what we lack
> We laugh, for what we have, are sorry.

As again:

> Our reasons are not prophets,
> When oft our fancies are.

Or once more:

> Let the event,
> That never-erring Arbitrator, tell us
> When we know all ourselves, and let us follow
> The becking of our chance.

It is all utterly like him.

There are other close similarities, of situation for example. Emilia speaks of her early playfellow, Flavina:

> like the elements
> That know not what, nor why . . .
> our souls
> Did so to one another: what she liked
> Was then of me approved; what not, condemned.
> The flower that I would pluck
> And put between my breasts –
> Oh, she would long
> Till she had such another, and commit it
> To the like innocent cradle.
> On my head no toy
> But was her pattern.

What is this but Hermia and Helena in *A Midsummer Night's Dream*? –

> All schooldays' friendship, childhood innocence:
> We, Hermia, like two artificial [artistic] gods,
> Have with our needles created both one flower,
> Both on one sampler, sitting on one cushion.

So in the late play we find Emilia saying:

> Cans't not thou work such flowers in silk?

When the rustics are to play before the Duke the weavers are to the fore (Bottom had been a weaver), and their rehearsing must be done in the woods. The schoolmaster ordains this, always good for a laugh in the plays, from the time when the playwright himself escaped from schoolmastering in the country.

> And, sweet companions, let's rehearse by any means
> Before the ladies see us – and do sweetly,
> An God knows what may come on't.

We remember Bottom's care not to frighten the ladies.

Again and again we can, if we have an ear, recognise the familiar voice, his turns of phrase, particular grand words: 'I am none that draw in the *sequent* trace.' 'Whose breath blows down the teaming Ceres' *foison* [a favourite word] ... whose hand *armipotent* from forth blew clouds the masoned turrets.'

> But when could grief
> Cull forth, as *unpanged* judgement can, fit'st time
> For best solicitation.

It is pure Shakespeare: the point is to be able to recognise it. The word 'unwappered', which means untired – he also uses the word 'wappered' – is West Midlands dialect, in case anybody supposes that he didn't come from Warwickshire.

Shakespeare was never afraid of repeating himself, or giving himself away – 'open, honest, and free'. 'As you are gentlemen', he says again here. He was always very conscious of what it meant to be a gentleman. This is what the word 'gentle' regularly applied to him at the time meant: it did not mean soft, it meant gentlemanly.

Quiller-Couch, good Shakespearean, made the point that Shakespeare was often his own source, and will recapitulate a situation or even a plot – not however, I think, characters: his fundamental interest, humanity. This ties in with what I have observed – that, though his observation of humanity and his imagination were universal, his range of experience was not wide: ranging between Stratford and London, and touring in southern England. Because so many of his plays have Italian subjects or flavouring, people conjecture whether he didn't go to Italy. It needs no accounting for: often the plots came from Italian sources, Bandello, Cinzio, Boccaccio, and he knew, rather close at hand, Florio and Emilia. The merchants of Venice are London merchants, save for their names.

Because he knew about the law, others have seen him inside a lawyer's office. They know nothing about the age: every man of property then needed to know some law. Conjecturers should shut up: there should be a close season for such people writing about him, confusing the innocent public. Because he knew about soldiering others have thought he *must* have been a soldier: Duff Cooper wrote a blithe piece of nonsense, *Serjeant Shakespeare*! I fear that the truth is that, once he got down to it, there was nothing but work.

As for *The Two Noble Kinsmen* I welcome once more being in line with tradition, though I find rather more of Shakespeare in it than I had expected.

In the 1970s I was approached by Crown Publishers of New York to collaborate in their imaginative venture of *The Annotated Shakespeare*. They had already had marked success with their *Annotated Dickens*, wanted to follow up with Shakespeare, and to recruit me for the venture. I had virtually made up my mind not to undertake yet another chore, when I was overpersuaded by a highly intelligent Australian editress. She took the trouble to come down to Cornwall to show me the fine expert lay-out of Illustrations, which were to be a chief feature of the edition. Here was something new, and that persuaded me.

For myself I regarded my participation as somewhat secondary. In all my publishing I have been ready to take a back-seat where Illustrations are concerned, willing to make suggestions, but regarding myself as no authority in this field. All this side of the venture was out of my hand, and was already being done for me. I appreciated the Illustrations like any other reader-user of the edition – indeed I was fascinated by them.

I had already had to give a lecture at the Metropolitan Museum in New York on 'Shakespeare and the Arts', but in this venture the accent was on productions of the Plays in the theatre. I have always been glamorised by theatre, without being the least bit professional (too much occupied by research); so privately I regarded these three large volumes as the best Illustrated Shakespeare available. As such this edition has particular value for all who like pictures and the stage, besides its utility for producers, amateur or professional.

With regard to the Annotations I concentrated my efforts on (a) checking them, (b) cutting them down. Slimming the Notes may not have pleased everybody, but I have always been against burying Shakespeare under a load of superfluous notes: a quarter of the page left to him, three-quarters of the page taken up by some unmemorable professor. Keep to what is necessary and relevant is my motto. This stood me in good stead when it came to *The Contemporary Shakespeare* not then contemplated.

The text of the Plays had already been decided for me – the reputable Globe edition which had long been regarded as standard. I should have preferred that of C. J. Sisson, whom I regard as my mentor in this field – for the reason I have given. He had an Elizabethan historian's familiarity with everyday usage from the documents, not the merely literary knowledge that is not only inadequate but can lead astray. It is typical of the inadequacy and unimaginativeness of the whole Shakespeare Industry that this best text is out of print and unobtainable, while money and energy are wasted on unnecessary ventures such as the new (and odd) Oxford Shakespeare.

As to my part in *The Annotated Shakespeare* (1978) I attach most importance to the Introductions I was called upon to write. This provided an opportunity to bring forward the great deal of new information I had accumulated over many years of research. Not critical argy-bargy by professors stifling Shakespeare. The only literary criticism I respect is that by minds on a level with the subject – Dr Johnson, Coleridge and Hazlitt, Walter Pater; and for dramatic criticism, those with experience of the stage, Granville Barker, Nevill Coghill.

My Introductions concentrate on what is factual and relevant: the date of the play, sources made use of, contemporary circumstances reflected or that sometimes suggested the work, reflections of Shakespeare's own experience (as with any other author) etc. Subsequently I was allowed to collect these Introductions conveniently in one volume, for English publication, as *Prefaces to Shakespeare's Plays*. Once more no use has been made of this volume by the professional trade-union, though it is full of new information such as only an Elizabethan historian can provide.

It is indeed obvious that such an historian has an essential contribution to make in the dating of the works. *The Annotated Shakespeare* is arranged in three volumes, Comedies, Histories, Tragedies; within each the opportunity is taken to arrange the Plays in the historian's proper chronological order.

7
The Contemporary Shakespeare

Having committed the offence, in the eyes of the Shakespeare Trade Union, of having solved all the problems of the Sonnets, biography, etc for them, I now proceeded to compound the offence. This was to edit *The Contemporary Shakespeare*, intended specifically for the benefit of the modern reader.[1]

Note, Reader, I do not need it for myself, it is intended specially for you. I can read the rebarbative old Tudor Teaschoppe spelling of the First Folio, printers' punctuation all over the place, misprints and mistaken interlineation, and all – as few can. I have been dealing with that sort of thing, Elizabethan documents and handwriting, most of my life.

You do not have to – no reason why you should. For, in fact, *all* editions of Shakespeare are modernised to some extent, it is simply a question of degree. Most editions modernise both the spelling and the punctuation; most of them correct mislineation in the old editions – or try to, for in fact none of the editors is a practising poet, and so is liable to get the scansion wrong. One Harvard professor, a friend of mine, made five mistakes in accenting words, in one edition of a play. He is not a practising poet. What is necessary, to carry the matter further for the benefit of the reader, is

---

[1] J.B.Bury modernised spelling and punctuation in his standard edition of Gibbon, though much nearer our own time. Note too his point that the authenticity of Procopius depends on '*the right determination of certain dates.*'

someone who is both familiar with Elizabethan language and usage, *and* a poet. Nothing less will do, and no-one else can do the job properly.

There is no doubt as to its *necessity*. For not only is Shakespeare's language four hundred years old – and a lot of it therefore archaic, out of use, and some of it no longer grammar today – but the gap between us and him is constantly increasing. So, to bring his language more in keeping with ours – where it can be done conservatively, with as little interference as possible, though where *necessary* – becomes ever more essential, to reader and viewer, in class, on stage, on television.

Remember, please, to keep open-minded. Try to read the First Folio if you like, or any other modern, conventional edition that is worthy of respect. I chiefly respect, and tend to follow, the textual work of Professor C.J.Sisson, his collected edition of all the works, along with his *New Readings in Shakespeare*.[1] For, like myself, he spent a life-time of research in Elizabethan documents, which express the actual life of the time, and so Shakespeare's usage was second nature to him, as it is with me. Among ordinary editions of individual plays, I like best *The Arden Shakespeare*,[2] though naturally some plays are better handled than others. Sisson's edition gives you admirable consistency.

What brought home to me, with rather a shock, the *necessity* of going a stage further with modernisation was when I learned in the United States that the younger generation was going off Shakespeare, because they could not take the archaic language. Anything rather than that they should drop Shakespeare! – such a loss to them. I learned this from several sources, not only from television, and from young people. An experienced publisher, in charge of bulk-purchases of Shakespeare for Roman Catholic High Schools, one-half of them right across the United States, corroborated what I had learned. He had encountered many classes that had simply dropped Shakespeare because they could not take the archaic language.

I thought, and think, this dreadful – and have come forward with a more modern edition, *The Contemporary Shakespeare*, to meet

[1] *William Shakespeare: The Complete Works*, ed. C.J.Sisson. Odhams Books, Ltd (out of print); C.J.Sisson, *New Readings in Shakespeare*, 2 vols., Cambridge Univ. Press.
[2] Published by Methuen.

the need.[1] Remember again, to be open-minded – this edition is intended only to help you. I have no objection to using any edition, provided it is a good one.

Here, again, my work is misunderstood by people of closed minds. From the beginning they were unable to understand that all my work on Shakespeare – Sonnets, biography, Plays – all the new findings and discoveries were, in a sense, *conservative*. They were all in keeping with tradition – Stratford, Warwickshire background, Southampton as patron, Marlowe the rival poet, the former mistress of the Lord Chamberlain, patron of Shakespeare's Company – one could not be more consistently traditional. I favour the early traditions about his teaching school for a time in the country, and the 'sportive' (his word) poaching the deer – no disgrace.

I am by nature conservative, loving tradition and disliking novelty of most kinds.

But conventional people cannot understand a conservative traditionalist who is open-minded. Let me tell them that conservatives are often much more open-minded than intellectuals wedded to their doctrines. Take the case of art and painting. In the old days of the Royal Academy traditionalists, most of them, were more ready to open the doors to 'modernists', than the latter are to the older school: these are much less tolerant. One can observe the same thing in architecture. All through Pevsner's Guides to the architecture of English counties, the international, modernist idiom is regularly preached up against any upholder of traditional styles – Comper or Lutyens, for example.

I have noticed the same thing in the United States. I once attended an exhibition where the paintings of Andrew Wyeth were twinned with the work of a modernist sculptor. I was taken in hand by a bright spark of *The New Yorker* who did not approve of my admiring 'old fashioned' Wyeth and shepherded me upstairs to see the (then) fashionable work of the sculptor – now forgotten. I took him back downstairs, and ushered him face to face with Wyeth's meticulous portrayal of a farm-cart, the wheel and spokes articulated with exquisite precision. 'Look', I said, 'you see, he can *draw*.'[2] This was not well received, and I was dropped.

[1] Published by the University Press of America, Washington, D.C., USA; distributed by Eurospan in Great Britain.
[2] cf. Giles Auty on 'the non-stop modernist assault on drawing and other worthwhile traditional practices in art schools.' *Spectator*, 13 Feb. 1988.

Similarly with my work on Shakespeare. They first couldn't take all the new findings and discoveries, or understand how traditional they were, completely consistent with what was *firmly* known before. Now, when they are having to accept all the new discoveries – for it is not possible to refute them – they will have equal difficulty in reconciling a conservative stance with an open-minded readiness to remove superfluous difficulties in the text of Shakespeare. (I may even be a reactionary, but an open-minded one: liberals are not – too doctrinaire.)

From the beginning I realised that my work would revolutionise our knowledge of Shakespeare. Historians know that in all revolutions there is a conservative element.

Paradoxically again, my attitude even to the text was a conservative one. Throughout all the plays I stuck to every line, every half-line, of the best text – usually Sisson's, compared with others – even though there is much mislineation, particularly in the later plays. That in itself gives one considerable freedom – no sacrosanctity where there is a good deal of doubt, leaving all editors freedom to choose. Here I was probably over-cautious. My governing principle with regard to archaic words was only to change a word when today people would not know its meaning.

To illustrate how conservatively this works out take the famous soliloquy in *Hamlet*, 'To be, or not to be.' There are 35 lines in that; only two present any difficulty for the modern reader:

> When he himself might his *quietus* make
> With a bare bodkin? Who would *fardels* bear . . .

An intelligent person might guess what *quietus* means, and an educated one ought to know: the word itself suggests 'quiet', or quittance, which is what it means. In Elizabethan times when you paid a bill, the receipt was given in Latin form, *quietus est*: it is quit, or paid. However, note that the word *quietus* has three syllables, so I replace it with the three-syllabled word, acquittance. One needs to be practised in scansion to do this job properly; others who have attempted it are not poets and cannot be trusted to get the scansion, or number of syllables, right.

The word 'bodkin' most women would know the meaning of –
it means a long hairpin or hatpin; so we may let that stand. Any
educated person who knows French – as all educated persons should
– will recognise 'fardels', from 'fardeaux', meaning burdens. However, nowadays most readers in the English-speaking world do not
know French, so we had better give it in English. Thus these two
lines read in my text:

> When he himself might his acquittance make
> With a bare bodkin? Who would burdens bear . . .

How can anyone reasonably object to those two words changed for
the benefit of the reader, out of the hundreds of words in those 35
lines?

Again let us be open-minded: if anyone has better suggestions to
make, very well. Secondly, I leave it open to change my own mind,
if I think of something better.

When *Romeo and Juliet* was first performed in my edition, at
Lynchburg College, Virginia, a member of the audience told me that
he had enjoyed it all the more *because he could understand every
word of it*. That was precisely the result I had in mind. Similarly,
the well-known Shakespearean producer, Joseph Papp, assured me
that 'when you hear it on the stage, you can't tell any difference.'
That again is the result I aim at: (a) the text so close to Shakespeare
that you can hardly tell any difference; yet (b) superfluous difficulties
removed, so that you can understand everything that is being said.

This does not mean that, at some points, considerable changes
are not absolutely necessary. Take the famous passage in *The Taming
of the Shrew* about the diseases of Petruchio's horse: it is

> possessed with the glanders and like to mose in the chine, troubled
> with the lampass, infected with the fashions, full of windgalls, sped
> with spavins, rayed with the yellows, past cure of the fives, stark spoiled
> with the staggers, begnawn with the bots, swayed in the back and
> shoulder-shotten; near-legged before, and with a half-cheeked bit and
> a headstall of sheep's leather [etc.]

What on earth could a modern reader, or hearer, be expected to
make of that? Richard Burton, fine Shakespearean actor, did a
memorable production of that play. When he appeared on the 'Today
Show' with me in New York he told us that they had had to cut

that piece out because no-one knew the meaning of it. He read the almost incomprehensible passage, and then followed it with my modernisation of it, of which he strongly approved. In fact he was favourable to the whole idea behind the work – actors and producers, engaged in the real work of presenting Shakespeare on the stage, being more flexible-minded and more generously disposed than professors and unqualified reviewers.

The first thing to notice is what only a scholar would know: there is no such word as 'mose' in the language. It is a misprint, the *Oxford English Dictionary* suggests for 'mourn', i.e. the horse is running, has a running sore in the chine. There are in fact many misprints, which we owe to the printers over the centuries: no sacrosanctity here, we must correct them. In later centuries, particularly in the eighteenth century, editors would often substitute their words for Shakespeare's, because they did not know or recognise the original Elizabethan. Sometimes I have even been so conservative, like Sisson, as to go back to an Elizabethan word which is still familiar enough.

Shakespeare's audience would know all those equine words – which we do not – or most of them. They were familiar with horse-flesh, as we are not – almost entirely dependent on horses for transport. Some of these words country folk, like myself, will know, so we do not need to replace all of them, only those we do not know, according to my guiding principle. Thus my rendering reads:

> possessed with glanders, and with a running sore in the back; troubled in the gums and infected in the glands; full of galls in the fetlocks and swollen in the joints; yellow with jaundice, past cure of the strangles; stark spoiled with the staggers, and gnawed by worms; swayed in the back and shoulder put out; near-legged before, with a half-cheeked bit and headgear of sheep's leather [etc.]

I hope that that at least makes the passage intelligible – my aim in all this. Further, it does away with the need for footnotes. A tremendous advantage of *The Contemporary Shakespeare* is that it reduces footnotes to a minimum. I can assure the reader that young people, others too, are put off by a text that occupies one quarter of a page and the footnotes three-quarters. Again, my rule is – a footnote only when necessary; for example, to translate a Latin, Italian or French phrase (of all of which Shakespeare had a sufficient working knowledge – only the ignorant think that he was uneducated). When it comes to the scenes almost entirely in French, in *Henry V*, I translate them in an Appendix.

Professors and teachers in class, members of the Trade Union, may fear that the reduction of footnotes to a minimum may reduce their own utility. However, there is so much in Shakespeare, a writer four hundred years old, that needs interpreting and explaining – if only they will devote themselves to what is really important, making the whole thing real and living, not deaden it with mere scholasticism.

I shelter myself behind the greatest of pure textual and bibliographical authorities, Sir Walter Greg. He has the bigness of mind to insist that what comes first is Shakespeare's thought and its expression; spelling, punctuation, mislineation etc are all secondary. We may add to that textual minutiae, except where meaning is concerned – and that is precisely what my edition provides. Those eminent textual authorities, Greg and my friend Fredson Bowers – who not infrequently differ about textual matters – are agreed that after all they are dealing only with probabilities. So what? – let us keep a sense of proportion – first things first; removing unnecessary difficulties in the way of our understanding the text. In that respect my task is in large part a negative one: there are plenty of difficulties in Shakespeare's thought and expression in themselves – very well, get rid of simple difficulties that are unnecessary, to concentrate on what is more important.

A New York friend – actually of the 'Today Show' – wrote that when he first heard of my project he was 'appalled', but when he read my explanation of it, he found it reasonable and persuasive. (I should hate anything unreasonable, I loathe what is erratic, and am not favourably inclined to the conjectural.) Professor Fredson Bowers himself, who has given us the best edition of Marlowe (attacked, unconvincingly, in the undependable *TLS*), was hesitant, but thought, if anybody could do the job, I might. *Verb. sap*.

Professor Bonnard pointed out the necessity of a modern text for foreigners years ago. I learned that at first hand from my friend Rouben Mamoulian, a producer of genius and a scholarly one, who gave us our first film version of *Vanity Fair* in colour, besides the grand film, *Queen Christina*. Mamoulian told me that, when young in Russia, he always found Shakespeare intelligible, for the translation was into a modern language. 'Here is the greatest English writer, whose language is clearly understood word by word, by every foreign nation in the world – but not by English-speaking people!'[1]

He has described for us his experience – valuable evidence. 'When I began to learn English, the greatest thrill I looked forward to was to read him in the original. This I did, but with a shocking result: I couldn't understand half of it. At first I attributed this to my insufficient knowledge of English. Later, when my English improved enough for me to enjoy and understand other great writers in English, I found that I still could not understand many of Shakespeare's words and expressions. So I buried myself in stacks of glossaries, dictionaries, footnotes, appendixes, and all sorts of research material. It took me a long time before I could honestly feel that I knew what every line in *Hamlet* meant, at least in terms of language. With this knowledge my appreciation of *Hamlet* increased a hundredfold.'

Since this was the experience of a theatre-man of genius, think what we have to gain – not that, on the other side, we have much to lose, perhaps a little flavour here and there. Mamoulian goes on that he worked away at *Hamlet* for several years. 'Working on it was one of the most exciting adventures of my life. But it is neither fair nor necessary to expect every reader to expend that much time and effort in order to enjoy *Hamlet* fully. Why not let him benefit by the research already done by many dedicated scholars? Why not go an important step farther – revise the text itself, replace all its archaisms and obscurities with words and expressions of modern English? Why not make it spontaneously intelligible to the present-day reader?'

Why not indeed?

Mamoulian spent years on *Hamlet*, and in the end came up with a drastically revised acting *version*. No notice of his useful and instructive effort was taken by the dumb professors, though I gave the book a warm welcome in that excellent paper, the *Wall Street Journal* – evidently not on their reading list. They never realise how much they lose from sheet blinkerdom. I suppose one should not expect too much from very ordinary talents, but if I learned from Mamoulian so could they. Shakespeare himself was one for learning everything from anybody everywhere – a perfect magpie for picking up hints and suggestions. Closed minds as usual had nothing to learn from

---

[1] *Shakespeare's 'Hamlet': A New Version*. Rouben Mamoulian, New York, 1965, 7–8.

this gifted man of the theatre, any more than from my unanswered and unanswerable discoveries.

We must make an exception here. It is significant that two minds that were open to these were both professionally addicted to theatre, my friends, Nevill Coghill and Robert Speaight. Actually Mamoulian went too far for me: his was an acting *version*, since he was a practical producer; he was willing to take short-cuts and make many cuts in the text. I have made no cuts whatsoever, but stuck to every line and half-line. Almost too conservatively, it might be argued, for many cases are open to option.

So *The Contemporary Shakespeare* must not be regarded as a version, or be referred to as such; it is just another *edition*, but a modern one. Modern education – or lack of it – being what it is, I am affronted by newspaper men referring to my 'rewriting' or even 'translating' Shakespeare! They don't know the difference. But what else can one expect of a 'pop-culture' without standards? The seventeenth and eighteenth centuries really did *rewrite* Shakespeare, but these people wouldn't know that, or appreciate the difference.

A contemporary edition has much to help reader, viewer, producer, actor on every page, at every point.

Take the simple matter of Accents. It is essential in speaking verse lines to know where the accent falls, how the word should be spoken to get the scansion right. Ordinary editions – since the editors are professors, not poets – are often all over the place in regard to accents, no help to anyone, since they can't help themselves. They can get so far as to accent a simple past tense or past participle, say 'languishèd' when the rhythm of the line demands it. Very often editions will distinguish by rendering this 'languish'd' when it is not accented, and 'languished', without the mark of an accent when the last syllable 'ed' is to be pronounced in full. Simplify! is my guiding principle throughout; thus when it is to be accented I mark it with an accent, so that there shall be no doubt. And, consistently with that, I have got rid of a host of apostrophes, 'languish'd', 'languish't', etc.

Most ordinary editions give you no help here. This is important, for Shakespeare characteristically is not consistent in his usage – so one is free to choose; or again, he will vary the accent in some cases, according to what the scansion demands.

No edition other than mine alerts actor and reader to the fact that some words that look like one syllable have to be pronounced as two. Such words as hour, fire, prayer, etc. In taking note of this I was corroborated by the fact that in old-fashioned New England speech such a word as prayer is still pronounced as two syllables – even such a word as 'there' is broken in two. So, in my edition, I give such words, where necessitated, a diaeresis: which means a 'mark over the second of two vowels to indicate that they are not one sound' (*Oxford Shorter Dictionary*). Thus: 'hoür', 'fïre', 'tïred', etc.

Far more frequent is the ending 'ion', in words like 'reputation'. The 'ion' has usually to be treated as two syllables; where it is, I have given it an accent to help, e.g. 'reputatiòn'. Educated actors, like Sir John Gielgud – no-one is closer in sympathy to Shakespeare's language – know this and act on it already. Lesser people, and younger actors, may not – and without the proper accentuation the rhythm of the line is lost. Here again Shakespeare's usage is not always consistent, and sometimes an accent is not necessary.

All this is simple enough, and presents no difficulty. But sometimes there is a complication, as when a word which we pronounce as two syllables has to be pronounced as three; for example, 'ocean', which has to be rendered with an accent to make it clear, 'oceàn'. The word 'puissant', gone out of use, was trisyllabic, so I have been able fortunately to replace it with 'powerful', which we must pronounced in turn as three syllables.

Quite a lot of Elizabethan usage is ungrammatical today, so we *must* correct and regularise that, like it or not. It was quite common to feature a plural subject with a singular verb:

> *Is* Bushy, Green and the earl of Wiltshire dead?

Is there any objection to correcting 'is' to 'are'? Surely not. Some modern editions already correct the original,

> These high wild hills and rough uneven ways
> Dra*ws* out our miles and make*s* them wearisome,

to 'draw' and 'make'. Then why not go further and regularise this Elizabethan usage consistently throughout? In any case the usage four hundred years ago was often inconsistent: linguistic usage has become more regular and consistent since then. Take, for example:

> Where is thy husband now? Where be thy brothers?

Nothing is lost by rendering this as we should today:

> Where is your husband now? Where are your brothers?

This brings us to the second person singular, for 'thou' requires should*est*, and would*est*, wil*t* and shal*t* and has*t*. All this has gone out of use: here a vast clearance and simplification can and should be made. This has the further advantage of getting rid of, or greatly reducing what is the ugliest sound in the language, 'st'. Note that it is quite difficult to pronounce when followed by 'th' – 'should*st th*ou' – and impossible for foreigners. Get rid of it when you can, for when the verb is in the past, or in the subjunctive, it requires a horrid collocation of consonants:

> Why usurpe*dst th*ou this?

When I told the young actors in Virginia performing *Romeo and Juliet* in our contemporary edition that at any rate I had delivered them from having to pronounce that, they cheered. It is enough to pronounce 'Why did you then usurp this?' Or 'Why would you then usurp this?'

When confronted by a former assistant at the Folger Shakespeare Library, discussing our *Contemporary Shakespeare*, he objected that changing 'thou' ('thee' and 'thine') was simply a 'trivial' change. 'But is it?', I replied. 'Every time you use 'thou' it requires the proper verb, second person singular: wilt, shalt, wouldest, shouldest, etc.' There are hundreds of cases of this all through the plays, hundreds of changes to make. This official had not thought the matter out – simply reached down the first objection that came to mind, without considering its grammatical consequences. Anything to negate or obstruct! Note here that Shakespeare used the modern form as well as the archaic. He did not write, 'O mistress mine, where ar*t th*ou roaming?' He wrote, 'where *are you* roaming?' And why? Probably for euphony: precisely what I have been pointing out – that it is not easy to pronounce 'th' after 'st' or 't'.

This same library assistant was able to tell the Press that the changes were made by someone without a knowledge of rhyme or scansion! Since I had been writing poetry all my life, I sent him, without comment, a copy of my *A Life: Collected Poems*. I have heard no more of *that* objection since. But the amount of obtuseness I have had to put up with its unbelievable: it would be laughable, if it were not sheer obscurantism, holding up knowledge when it is for the less intelligent to learn. They lose so much by it.

Like the former MacManaway of that same institution, who thought that 'Never shall we know who the young man of the Sonnets, or who the Rival Poet was.' The unpardonable thing about the less intelligent is that *they do not want to know*, when they need to most of all. This again has a sociological aspect. It is at last being realised how much dead wood there is in the universities, people with permanent tenure who show little interest in their subject and contribute nothing to it.

How little they care for literature is witnessed when, at one provincial university, the 'uncooked' poetry of the media today is made required reading for students – a Redgrove rather than an accomplished poet like Betjeman, let alone great poets like Robert Bridges or Kipling. Once more, if Kipling was good enough for T.S. Eliot, he is certainly good enough for *them*.

Inflation lowers the value of the currency: the post-war academic inflation has lowered educational standards not only in provincial universities but, as everybody knows, throughout the schools. Even at Oxford a trendy professor of Eng. Lit. prefers the nonsense of the Puritan Ranters to the Caroline Poets – no idea of quality, or caring for it. Where equality rules quality goes.

We should take every opportunity to get rid of the ugliest sound in the language, 'st'. Naturally non-writers are apt to be insensitive about such matters: I have been struck by the aural insensitiveness of ordinary academics almost as much as by their visual insensitiveness. My friend William Cooper, admirable novelist, has waged a lifelong campaign against 'among*st*' and 'whil*st*'. Why use these ugly words when 'among' and 'while' are there to serve the purpose? Throughout *The Contempoary Shakespeare* I have remedied that.

We no longer use the archaic third-person singular either, 'hath' and 'doth', 'thinketh' etc. So replace those superfluities complicating the text with the regular modern usage, 'has', 'does', 'thinks' etc. We no longer use 'be' for the third person plural either: we use 'are' regularly – as in that line above, 'Where be thy brothers?', we should say 'Where are your brothers?'

A larger class of changes comes about by ridding the text of subjunctives. Today we rarely use the subjunctive, except occasionally after 'if'; even in modern English we say 'if it is' far more often than 'if it be', and I suspect that the latter is on its way out entirely. But in Elizabethan times it was frequent – not only after 'if' but after 'though', 'until', 'lest', 'although', 'unless', 'whether' etc. Thus we get rid of hundreds of unnecessary subjunctives from the text. We no longer use them. Why should foreigners in learning English have this useless obstacle to get over? English is the world's language today, and Shakespeare is naturally much used in learning it. We should therefore clear *unnecessary* difficulties out of the way, and we *must* change what is positively ungrammatical.

Elizabethans used a double negative frequently to emphasise its force: 'Nor should you not think neither' – actually there are three negatives there. One is the rule today. Similarly with double comparatives – 'more worser', 'most evillest'; we reduce to 'worse', 'most evil', etc. Anything unnecessarily complex it is better to simplify.

We come to a class of words that have changed their meaning after four hundred years, some of them into the exact opposite, so that we *must* change them. When Hamlet says, 'I'll make a ghost of him that *lets* me', he means 'stops', and we should change it accordingly to get it right. The word 'presently' in those days meant 'immediately', 'at once', not just in a minute or two, as we take it. Since 'presently' has three syllables, those replacements will not do, for 'immediately' has five, 'at once' only two; so we can say 'instantly' or 'now at once'.

Shakespeare uses the word 'owe' where we use 'own' – the meaning has changed. So we should change it: not much difference of sound between 'owe' and 'own'. Take the line,

> Thou dost here usurp the name thou ow'st not:

we should replace with

> You do here usurp the name you own not.

And this gives us the bonus of getting rid of two ugly 'st's. Altogether a considerable number of words have changed their meanings. 'Prevent' then had its Latin meaning, to go before, or forestall, rather than to hinder or stop outright. The word 'still' is often used to mean 'ever', 'always'. And so on.

We come to a class of archaic words that may conveniently be changed; since they are of one syllable and do not make the slightest difference to the scansion they may readily be replaced. 'Sith' for since, 'wrack' for wreck, 'holp' for helped, 'bare' for bore. Why retain 'brake' for broke, 'spake' for spoke, 'writ' for wrote? No point in it. In fact 'he wrote it' is more euphonious and more pronounceable than 'he writ it'.

Again, open-mindedness should be our guiding principle. If it is necessary occasionally to retain an archaic form for the sake of a rhyme, I have no objection to doing so. It occurs, not very frequently, that we need to retain 'thee' or 'thine' for the sake of a rhyme. Very well, then let us retain it: we do not want a wooden consistency, we can afford to be pragmatic, especially as the need arises only occasionally.

We should, however, favour consistency where it is obviously preferable. In Elizabethan times the relative pronouns 'who' and 'which' were interchangeable; we distinguish between 'who' for persons and 'which' for objects. Shakespeare uses them in the Elizabethan way, interchangeably; but, somewhat oddly to our ear, he uses the personal 'who' more frequently for impersonal objects, rivers, buildings, towns, and then 'which' for persons. It is a help to everybody to conform here to modern usage, and we do so throughout *The Contemporary Shakespeare*.

Two words, regular in his time, cause unnecessary confusion. Elizabethans used the word 'cousin' generically to include nephews. So, when the malign Richard III refers to his nephews, whom he had murdered in the Tower, as 'cousins' we should correct it for the benefit of the reader. Similarly 'niece' was used for grand-daughter – in his will Shakespeare referred to his grandchild Elizabeth as such: regular enough four hundred years ago, we must correct it for today. There are pointless archaisms in spelling which we should modernise also. What is the point of spelling 'vild' for vile, 'yond' for yon? Anything lost by replacing such words?

So far all has been plain-sailing, fairly simple. We come to something more problematical with completely archaic words, words of which we no longer know the meaning. There are many of these. Of course we could annotate as ordinary editions do, and half-fill the page with footnotes for our eyes to range up and down and lose the place or, worse, concentration. On the whole, it is better to replace them. Sometimes this is easy, when the archaic word has the same number of syllables and accent as the modern. The word 'coistrel' appears only a couple of times: it means rascal. 'Coil' means fuss: 'bisson' means purblind or blinding. Just as well to replace them.

A number of these ancient out-of-use words do not have equivalents in number of syllables or accents: 'moldwarp' for mole, 'chopine' for high-heeled shoes, 'crants' for garland, though one could say wreath, or simply flowers. Then too Shakespeare coined quite a number of words which have not survived. In his grand way with words he was particularly fond of ending words with '-ure': 'rondure', 'expressure', for example. These two give no difficulty, one can say circuit and expression. Is the word 'momentany' a coinage, or is it merely a misprint for momentary? I shouldn't be surprised if it were (if I may be forgiven a modern subjunctive); anyhow we should replace the 'n' by 'r' – any great harm in that? 'Intendment' is a word of his: intention will do for us.

Oddly enough, it is the simplest words that give most difficulty. Redundant words, for example: Elizabethans said 'an' for if, but also 'an if' where we say only if; they frequently said 'if that', where we regard 'that' as redundant. In replacing these we have often to add a syllable in place of it. This is not always necessary, however. As Shakespeare grew older his verse became freer, the scansion far more lax – and this leaves us much more scope. In the earlier plays the blank verse is regular, the lines end-stopped, and one must adhere to the scansion. As the verse becomes more relaxed so one has greater freedom of movement; until, in the end, no wonder compositors sometimes had difficulty in telling whether it was verse or prose. Scholars know that in late Shakespeare the unit is often a verse-paragraph, the line frequently ending with prepositions. As with the last period of great painters – Tintoretto, Titian, Rembrandt – one thinks impressionism is all.

Simple adjurations, expletives, swear-words give great difficulty. What are we to do with the word 'whoreson', so frequent on the lips of coarse fellows in those days? The American s.o.b. (son-of-a-bitch) would be the nearest equivalent; but the British do not use the expression, nor would it scan. On the other hand, Americans do not use our swear-word 'bloody', in that sense – with them the word has its literal meaning. I don't like to confess myself defeated in this realm, but have usually been reduced to British usage.

The frequent apostrophe 'Marry!', used as an invocation, gives no difficulty. Historically it refers back to the Virgin Mary, and appears again in the phrase, 'Marry, come up!' It has now gone out, though Sir Charles Oman at All Souls told me that Lady Oman heard it in the 1914–18 war. A soldier's wife she was visiting in an Oxford back-street said suddenly, 'Marry come up! Here's John.' I should have loved to hear that bit of Elizabethan speech on twentieth-century lips. However, it is not difficult to replace it, according to context, with 'Indeed!' or 'For sure' – I haven't dared to be so modern as to say, 'Hullo!'

There are Elizabethan salutations, like 'God 'ild you' for God shield you, or 'Godden' for Good even. 'God's wounds!' was Elizabeth I's favourite swear-word. In Victorian novels this appears as 'Zounds' – I have never heard it on anyone's lips. For all these things we have to find equivalents.

Malapropisms offer greater difficulty. These are words used mistakenly by ignorant people, dredged up by the author for comic effect, as when Mistress Quickly declares that she is in a 'canary' for quandary. I do not know if Shakespeare was the inventor of this comic ploy, but he certainly was its chief patentee on the lips of Bottom the weaver, Dogberry and Verges, Pompey and Elbow, Dame Quickly, and other lower-class people. Sometimes here I put the correct word in brackets, for the benefit of the reader – even more necessary for a foreign reader – and, if it needs further elucidation, I sometimes go so far as a footnote.

Lastly, what ought we to do with the shortenings and apostrophes with which conventional texts are so liberally sprinkled, starred or – as I sometimes think – scarred? All those 'i's' or 'i'th's' for in or in the, 'o's or 'o'th's for of or of the. Usually I have lengthened these, normalised them for the reader, especially where no difficulty for scansion arises – and this is usually the case in the later plays where they are most frequent.

In any case, in these as in other matters actors have a great deal of latitude. Much depends on their intelligence, and on their training and practice in speaking Elizabethan verse. The generation before me, headed by such reformers as William Poel, brought about a great improvement in this regard, compared with the rhetorical oratory of the Victorians, the over-emphasis of such actors as Sir Henry Irving.

This is comparable with what Shakespeare himself effected in his career as actor and producer, as we can tell from the detailed instructions Hamlet gives to the players. The whole burden of these is to hold the mirror up to nature, be natural, gestures appropriate to the words, no over-emphasis. It is clear that he modernised earlier Elizabethan over-rhetorical effects, the rhetoric of Tamburlaine for example, stomping about the stage. Never, then, shall we see actors more closely in the spirit of Shakespeare than in my generation, with Gielgud and Olivier, Edith Evans and Peggy Ashcroft.

8
Criticism

More nonsense has been written about William Shakespeare than about any other writer. I suppose we ought not to be surprised at that: since he is the world's writer he is a chief target of the world's silliness. But I am not wasting time in this book on the dolts who would like to think that his works were written by anybody but himself. This book is concerned with academics and intellectuals whose duty it is to learn and teach, though too often they fall down on it – as we have seen all through with the Shakespeare establishment, or industry, perhaps trade union would be more exact.

Not all of these, however, were obtuse or obstructive from the beginning. At Oxford Professor F. P. Wilson, as we have seen, was warmly welcoming. Shortly afterwards he died, a great loss to me, leaving me to face the music. I have often thought since that, if my solution of the problems was good enough for him – most conservative and reliable of Shakespeare scholars – it was good enough for the lesser fry.

We must be fair. There were others who saw the point, even at Oxford. J. I. M. Stewart wrote: 'Dr Rowse is a poet as well as an historian – and it is really the poet who has written a very good book about Shakespeare. Not only does he draw a splendidly rich and vivid background for the dramatist; he also shows, again and again, how the passion and excitement of the age pours into the plays.' I am particularly glad of this witness, for the Eng. Lit. trade union have been only too ready to dismiss my work as that of only an historian, 'not in the field', as one not very bright young fellow put it. Perhaps it is an unfair advantage to be both historian *and* poet, when they do not appreciate the rarity of the conjunction. (It is more Elizabethan than modern: witness Samuel Daniel or Ralegh.)

Outside Oxford Professor Kenneth Muir was good enough to declare: 'When all criticisms have been made, the book remains the best account so far of Shakespeare the Man.' The professor then administered a professorial admonition: 'if only Mr Rowse could have toned down his cocksureness he could have written a master-piece.' But how otherwise could it be brought home to them what a mess they had left the subject in? I was indeed quite confident that my conclusions were correct, as against their muddled uncertainty.

This raises an interesting general question. The *reader* will recognise that, after a lifetime of writing, I know quite well what I am doing, what others are up to, what they think, and why they think it. It is the conventional thing to depreciate oneself to others. But I do not much respect convention, or conventional people. In literary matters you must not betray confidence, you are supposed to express a demure diffidence. Early on I was reproved over this by a regular Sunday reviewer, Raymond Mortimer, who was generous about *A Cornish Childhood*, but thought that the proper thing was to write oneself down to catch others out. I knew as well as the next man that this was the middle-class Public School line; but I was neither middle-class nor Public School, and I was not going to conform to their rule, and in fact I never have. Any more than Ernest Bevin would. ('I'm a turn-up in a million.' He was.)

I thought the convention too boring, and a not very subtle psychological point arises here. As La Rochefoucauld brings out, depreciating yourself is only a way of boosting yourself to others: it flatters their self-esteem. Cyril Connolly had a regular ploy of writing himself down: it was only a way of writing himself up. John Betjeman always affected humility: 'I'm no good. I'm only an emmet', etc. With him there was a genuine element of lack of self-confidence – quite unjustified, and I never encouraged it. I don't suppose that he had read La Rochefoucauld, but Connolly might have done. This was the technique by which he gained popularity – became a member of 'Pop' – at Eton, and he continued to employ it all his life. It is a way of flattering people, and people are fools to fall for it.

I find it a bore, and think it beneath me to play their game. It is simpler to have a proper estimate of one's own quality (and defects: I know mine better than any reviewer can tell me). Besides this it saves time, and clears the way for the work itself. Connolly constantly moaned that he could not get done what he really would like to have written. I was never taken in, or even interested, by his constant self-denigration. I credited him with a streak of genius, a *poète manqué*, with a real passion for literature.

He welcomed my book – without, I think, really grasping its point; for he was not a historian,[1] nor in the real sense a scholar – he was not dedicated enough for that. The result was that he was oddly uncertain about Shakespeare. Quite a lot of clever people are. It is my job to set them right – and what a job it has been! (I take the reader into my confidence.)

For fun the reader may like to know what some of the clowns of the popular press thought. Malcolm Muggeridge, though making some condescending concessions – 'it is perfectly true of course that he knows a great deal about the Elizabethan age ... there is much to be learnt from his pages about the background to Shakespeare's life and work ... given a proper humility', etc – concentrated on a personal attack on the author. Rather a joke to think of a Muggeridge giving lessons in humility, but did he know anything about the Elizabethan age? He was 'confirmed in his opinion by estimable authorities like Mr Ivor Brown and Professor Dover Wilson.'

Ivor Brown was a fellow journalist who had a fixation on the view that the Dark Lady was Mary Fitton – of the blue eyes and auburn hair, in trouble with young Pembroke, who was twelve when the Sonnets begin, urging the young man to marry and carry on the family! Nonsense, of course – and Ivor Brown didn't welcome my putting his book out of court. It is a *duty* for a scholar to tell the public when there is rubbish cluttering up the ground. I repeat it: most of the mountain of stuff written about Shakespeare *is* rubbish, and people should save themselves the trouble of reading it.

Dover Wilson was quite another matter from the journalist Ivor Brown: he was at least a Shakespeare scholar. He had real insights into the text, but let his imagination run away with him. I would

---

[1] We were exact contemporaries at Oxford: ironically he was a History Exhibitioner at Balliol while I was the English Literature Scholar at Christ Church. He should never have taken the History School, in which he got a Third Class.

never have dared to take the risks he did, re-writing stage-directions enthusiastically, as if he were producer-director! Enthusiasm was his characteristic quality; it had some advantages as well as disadvantages: it meant that he was keen on the theatrical approach, a recommendation for an academic.

But the risks he took! There is his notorious explanation of Hamlet's insult to Ophelia: 'Get thee to a nunnery! why woulds't thou be a breeder of sinners?' Dover Wilson would have us think that Hamlet meant by 'nunnery' a brothel! Clean contrary to the common sense of the passage. Here, reader, is a point of general application: always take the meaning of a passage simply and directly, before looking for esoteric meanings. And, by the way, the passage provides us with an example of that deplorable sound, 's't', followed by a 'th', difficult for English speakers, let alone foreigners. Why not render it simply: 'why would you be a breeder of sinners?'

It was a pity that Dover Wilson knew no better than Ivor Brown, when it came to the Sonnets. He had never noticed that Mr W. H. was Thorp's man, not Shakespeare's, and was under the usual misapprehension that Mr W. H. was Shakespeare's young man. He therefore plumped for Pembroke. Again, no common sense. When he said that he was 'so far along that line', in his edition for the *Cambridge Shakespeare*, that he could not go back on it, this shocked me – as it would any historian. We are dedicated to saying what is true. If anyone should discover that the half-Italian-Jewish Emilia Bassano was a flaxen-haired Scandinavian, I should be the first person to say then she would not have been the Dark Lady.

Hence Dover Wilson's edition of the Sonnets provides yet another example of confusion, mixing up people's minds, as practically all editions hitherto have done. The great majority of scholars from Malone onwards have seen quite clearly that the man in the Sonnets was the obvious person, the young patron – but they did not see how to explain the dedication. As the first to explain it, I did not realise that it would be difficult for others to follow. No reason why I should not stake my claim, since others have not the generosity to admit it, and cannot bear – as Roger Prior points out – to admit that they were wrong.

The *Times Literary Supplement*, having put its money on the wrong horse (not *The Times* itself, which backed me), lay low about Dover Wilson's edition and did not review it. I was waiting in my lair for that: the public should be informed of the truth of the matter. The upshot was that the *Cambridge Shakespeare* is having to re-edit the Sonnets by another hand. I expect that it will get half the new findings right, and wobble over the rest, or get them wrong.

We need not waste time on the attacks of the professional media men – a Muggeridge or Michael Foot, just a politician (not a very good one even at that). Or on a blast from a journalist like Bernard Levin, who wished to think that 'the main question remains open, and will continue to do so until we find Shakespeare's manuscripts, or better still his diary.' That shows that the journalist has no idea how things are about the Elizabethan age: that there are none of the manuscripts of Shakespeare's plays remaining (except for a few pages from a projected play about Sir Thomas More). As for a diary – a Levin would not know that very few Elizabethan diaries exist, nor that we have something unique in the way of autobiography in the Sonnets. There is a general point here again for the reader: these media men are betraying their trust to the public. It is their business to inform the public what the facts are. When they do not know them, they should acquaint themselves with them; if they do not understand them, then they should try to – they might even ask.

An American literary scholar wrote to me: 'this afternoon I received my copy of the *Times Literary Supplement* and was appalled at the nastiness of that review.' This was that of their regular Shakespeare 'expert', John Crow. Christopher Sykes, a real writer, described this, in the New York *Nation*, as 'a long article of some 3500 words in furious hostility. It was muddled thunder. His point of view, except that it was hostile and that he adopted the silly superior tone of the anonymous reviewer, was never made clear, and he wrote with sly, roundabout affectation.'

In Canada Dr Sidney Fisher, who possessed all four Shakespeare folios and knew more than anyone about the topography of Elizabethan London, wrote: 'I am sure that you will be bitterly attacked by some of the current generation. You have shown them up as lacking precise knowledge, judgment in human affairs and analytical power, and I am sure they will not forgive you.' He concluded: 'with a single book you have put yourself at a great distance ahead of everyone else who has written on Shakespeare, biographers and critics alike.

Part of the reason for this, it is clear, is your competence as an historian; and I perceive from your comments on the literary gentlemen from whom the other books have come that you also understand this point.'

I did, and do, indeed – and as a good Celt, have not forgiven it. Here was the impression it made on a simple outsider, an unknown correspondent who wrote to me guilelessly: 'myself had always found the Sonnets almost mysterious in their cross allusions, cryptic words and dedication. I also followed the various back-biting letters in *The Times*, finding them most bitchy beyond expectation.' This innocent evidently had no idea what a snake-pit academic and literary life is. I am not so much shocked by that, I know its denizens too well: what shocks an historian is that *they do not want to know*. Then, when they are told, they resent it. I do not find this worthy of respect: what else are they for, but to learn before they presume to teach?

Let us return to the supposed Shakespeare 'experts'.

At Stratford the ranking 'authority' was Professor Terence Spencer, who combined being head of the Shakespeare Institute with being professor at Birmingham University. His treatment of my book makes an interesting study. He welcomed the historical chapters on Elizabethan Warwickshire, Stratford, and Shakespeare's early social environment. 'The voices are heard; the human beings of a departed generation live and move; the characters flicker for a moment, memorably, in the dark backward and abyss of time.' Still it is a give-away that he thought I had got my historical material from the purely literary colleagues whom he cited: no idea that he was dealing with an historian to whom the Elizabethan age was his life-long study. He evidently did not know my books on the subject.

When he came to the literary part of my book he let himself go, and exposed himself. Like the rest of them he thought that there were no solutions to the problems of the Sonnets, *therefore* they were insoluble. He can easily be shown to have been wrong. Recall that I had been able to date the Sonnets firmly to 1591–4. This was in keeping with traditional opinion that held (rightly) that the Sonnets were contemporary with *Venus and Adonis*, 1593 and *The Rape of Lucrece*, 1594. However, no-one had the knowledge to prove this from the consistent topical references.

Now Sonnets 78 to 85 deal with the appearance of the Rival Poet, and are all in the present tense: the rivalry is on-going. With Sonnet 86, the rivalry suddenly ends: it is practically all in the past tense, the rival is never mentioned again.

> Was it the proud full sail of his great verse . . .
> Was it his spirit, by spirits taught to write
> Above a mortal pitch, that struck me dead? . . .
> But when your countenance filled up his line,
> Then lacked I matter, that enfeebled mine. [etc]

Everything in these Sonnets blazed forth Marlowe – everyone knew that it was his 'mighty line' (Jonson's phrase for it) that had contributed great poetry to the drama. I had shown that the two poets were closer than anyone had realised and that they were well aware, from the echoes in the verbiage, of each other's works – *Venus and Adonis* and *Hero and Leander*.

And, by the way, what were they rivalling each other for? – The patronage of the patron, i.e. the Sonnets were written for the patron. So much for the obtuse, like the ineffable Professor Wilson Knight, who could not see anything of the patron in the speaking likeness of him portrayed, family, circumstances at the time, and all.

Very well, Christopher Marlowe was killed on 30 May 1593: this is what that Sonnet 86 is referring to, with an indirect, but recognisable, reference to his *Faustus* thrown in. Professor Terence Spencer couldn't see this. 'Unfortunately the new argument – that the rival poet must have been dead because Shakespeare uses the past tense of the verb at the beginning of Sonnet 86 – is a mistaken interpretation of the syntax of the poem.' There are *ten* verbs in the past tense in the short space of those fourteen lines – couldn't the professor *count*? Why couldn't he keep an open mind instead of getting it wrong?

It is sad to have to charge the professor with stupidity; but his eagerness to reject my solutions led him to make a stupid mistake. 'Against stupidity', said Schiller, 'the gods themselves struggle in vain.' This is the kind of thing one has had to put up with from these Shakespeare 'experts' all along. Now *not a single one of their objections has stood up, not one of my findings and discoveries ever answered*.

Professor Spencer was equally at sea about my dating of *A Midsum-*

mer Night's Dream.[1] Professor Madeleine Doran was a good, academic Shakespearean, and a friend of mine. With the kindliest intention, she showed me her edition of *A Midsummer Night's Dream* in which the Countess of Southampton's marriage to Heneage was included with half-a-dozen other marriages up and down the 1590s, as if they were all the same case! Her edition was no worse than other people's: they all took this line (Chambers included) throwing up half-a-dozen names as if *in pari materia*. I doubt if they know what the term means: it means equally comparable.

These suggested marriages, thrown up in the air, are *not* equally comparable: only one marriage, that of the patron's mother, is in accordance with all the circumstances, characters and dating.

It is just like their thinking of Emilia Bassano as *in pari materia* with any other name they may think up as 'candidate' for Dark Lady. She is no 'candidate': she is the one and only woman.

A Professor J. Isaacs, an Eng. Lit. professor at one of the lesser colleges in London, was able to pronounce that my work was 'universally condemned'. From that the reader may judge the state of the case – and who remembers who this unenlightened person was now? One thing that has never ceased to surprise me is that these people have no idea of their own rating, and whom they are trying to counter. No sense of humour, I suppose – though professorial conceit is a familiar feature throughout academic life, while envy is a vocational disease. 'Base Envy' – as the poet Thomson says,

> hates that excellence it cannot reach.

In a kindly meant letter William Empson from Cambridge explained the case to me. 'I am sure that your broad position is the right one, and I readily sympathise with your irritation against the Eng. Lit. establishment. But I think that, in its slow self-regarding way, it had been coming round for some time to accept what you and I consider the right view on this matter. The objection to your publications is one which would be felt in any University Department, if a man claimed he had found how to stop a tooth, and nobody had done it before.'

But the reader can see for himself that in fact nobody *had* stopped these teeth before, and the real root of their objection was that some-

---

[1] v. earlier, pp. 72–3.

body had done it for them. Empson went on, 'you must please realise they all think you tell these lies[!] in order to make money by cheating the people who buy your books.'

I can hardly think so ill of them as that – Empson was liable to exaggerate. All the same I was shocked. For it is the life-blood of an historian to tell the truth – that is all he cares for, to find it out the inspiration of his work. That is what leads us researchers on – *we want to know*. These other people apparently do not – fancy allowing yourself to be put off because someone of authority was confident in his findings!

As for sales of my books, the case here also is otherwise. They would have sold far better if I had adhered to the conventional line that prevails about Shakespeare, in the universities and elsewhere, and submitted by work to their 'better judgment' (Heaven forfend!) Witness my experience with my Introduction to the *Riverside Shakespeare* – invited to write it, to have it turned down by the Trade Union. Think what these people deprive their students of, and what standards they exhibit!

Funnily enough, I care less about that than they would realise. They wouldn't know that a real writer, fundamentally, writes for an audience of one – *what he really cares about is the subject in and for itself*: not what other people think about it or him. I have long ago arrived at a solipsist position in the confusion of present-day society and its standards. If people choose to read my books, they are free to do so; but that is not my motive for writing them. I write to please myself, because I am fascinated by the subject, whatever anybody thinks, anxious to get it right.

The business-minded Professor Schoenbaum, who was entering into competition, described my work as merely 'a triumph of promotion'. No idea of what my work was contributing to the subject, not only the definitive solutions to the problems of the Sonnets, but to the dating and circumstances of plays, the significance of Shakespeare's social and political thinking – *there* was something new. Later on he came to the view that Emilia Bassano *might* even be the Dark Lady. I expect that, by this time, he knows that she was.

In view of all this I cannot accept the judgment of an expatriate Oxford professor, Christopher Ricks, who wrote later that if I had not been so aggressive, they would have 'followed me like lambs'. I simply do not believe it. I do not think it would have made the slightest difference, in their inspissated obtuseness, determined to stick in their old rut. How could one have been any other than aggressive when confronted by such opposition, such stupidity? It was a duty to describe it for what it was. I know no such barricade of misdirection and misjudgment erected in the field of plain historical writing. Historians set a better example in seeking to know the facts and recognising error.

At the Huntington Library where I embarked on my Shakespeare work friends advised me not to waste time in controversy. Occasionally I corrected a fact, or a mis-statement, like those in the *Times Literary Supplement*. But, for the most part, I kept plodding on with the work. My friends there may not have known how I would react – most people would have taken the line of least resistance and given up. I did not consider that for a moment: that would have left the third-rate in possession of the field, and the subject in the mess in which I found it.

Though sickened by it, I was fortified by a similar experience years earlier. I felt that I had been through it all before – over Appeasement, in politics. In the 1930s, when I was a political candidate, practically the whole country was bent on following Neville Chamberlain in 'appeasing' Hitler. Fancy people being such idiots as to think that Hitler was a man of peace!

One doesn't need to argue the matter now, it is all settled. But it always *was* obvious! People wouldn't listen, they wouldn't take telling. Young as I was, I kept up a regular campaign of warning, articles, speeches, letters to *The Times*.[1] And was, of course, for the most part discountenanced. Lord Lothian, an infatuated Appeaser, was good enough to controvert the young scholar. His chief friend at All Souls, Lionel Curtis, said 'Philip died, in the Washington Embassy, in the knowledge that he had been wrong.' Any fool should have been able to see that Hitler meant war.

One of the current younger generation, Lord Egremont, asked me to explain why people were so bent on being wrong. I gather too that the younger generation of Germans want to know why the previous generation was so obtuse about Hitler. The answer is quite simple: *people believe what they want to believe*. I go further: people in the mass are incapable of thinking; their thinking is practical or

[1] For the historical record I published what I had written *at the time* – as few else could – in *The End of an Epoch*.

technical: they can mend a fuse, but they cannot think in the abstract. By the end of the 1930s, ill with it all, I was prepared for the consequences of their idiocy. I continue to observe it, looking round the world today, like Jonathan Swift – or William Shakespeare – on the varieties of human folly.

It is the proper business of intellectuals to think things out, to think straight, not to pander to popular prejudices. I do not claim much credit for having been right about Appeasement – any ordinary intelligence should have seen what Hitler was up to. But, for the most part, people whose business it was to know, the authorities, government and politicians alike, would not listen – any more than Shakespeare 'experts' will.

The chief 'authority' at Harvard, Professor Harbage, could not see the point. We have seen that his 'standard' work, *Shakespeare's Audience*, has been shown to be wrong in its assumptions and grasp of the facts. Nor was he going to learn from me: 'I must continue to distinguish probabilities from facts. Of course there will never be any unanimity of opinion on what constitutes a "reasonable doubt".' That *sounds* reasonable enough; but when you think it out, you realise that it is not reasonable to carry doubt beyond the point where there is no reason for it. Historians know when certainty is more reasonable – i.e. where *all* the circumstances are consistent, cohere and corroborate each other, and not a single fact can be found to contradict it.

To be fair, these people probably cannot tell the difference: they are not intellectually equal to it. Harbage's successor at Harvard still has 'doubts'; he thinks that Emilia Bassano might well be a 'candidate'! The library assistant who thought that I had no ear for rhyme or scansion now thinks that Roger Prior's further corroboration of Emilia Bassano, 'does indeed offer some new connections to ponder with respect to your identification ... and if those connections are more than coincidental it also provides some interesting associations with the rest of the Shakespearean canon'!

'Connections', 'associations' – he has got as far as that along the road! Churchill said of Abraham Lincoln that people couldn't see moral courage when it stared them in the face. Myself, I can tell third-rate thinking when confronted with it.

I had explained all my earlier findings to Louis Auchincloss, then a friend, and thought that he understood them. When his book on the Sonnets, *Motiveless Malignity*, came out I was astonished to find that it simply repeated the conventional nonsense now exposed as such. He could at least have learned better.

My reply to this book was that Auchincloss would know about the writing of novels, and also about American law (he was a professional lawyer), as I did not: I would expect him to tell me on those subjects. But, over the Elizabethan age, I would expect him to listen to what I had to say. What was unreasonable about that?

He wrote back an angry reply: he could not tell me anything about novel-writing or American law. This was simply bad logic: he clearly knew *more* about both, for I know nothing about either. I saw at once that, whatever his claims as a novelist, this was second-rate intellectually, a purely emotional reaction. Intellectually, we may regard him as the loser – there was so much he could have learned. As it is, the book, *Motiveless Malignity*, is without value.

Altogether I have had much to put up with for sticking to my guns, when I could have taken a much easier option – and been wrong, like the experts who wouldn't take telling from Harvey about the circulation of the blood.

9
'Experts' and Media-men

I suppose some of those recalcitrant doctors may have been friends of Harvey's – and I did not find my friends any more helpful, for the most part. My work was certainly not treated with favouritism, very much the reverse. My oldest friend at Oxford was Lord David Cecil. He never exerted himself to express an opinion about my Shakespeare work, beyond saying that it *might* be right. He never took the trouble to go into it, and see for himself. I knew him intimately, and that he would never stick his neck out to get into trouble of any sort. He went out of his way to avoid controversy (even when attacked by the Leavises). So I did not expect him to speak up for me: though always anxious for me to review his books, he never reviewed one of mine. I am not reproaching him but, as a ranking professor at Oxford, with my discovery in the Bodleian of all places, he should at least have gone into the subject.

Oddly enough, I do not like controversy either: it wastes time. People describe my work as 'controversial', when they really mean controverted. My views about Appeasement were not controversial, though they were constantly controverted: they were in fact correct. Similarly I do not regard my findings about Shakespeare as 'controversial'.

My most highly decorated pupil was Dame Veronica Wedgwood, O.M., Dame of the (former) British Empire, etc. She was an early favourite pupil; so, coming back on the plane together from New York, I explained to her that I had found the problems of the Sonnets to work out intelligibly and consistently. To my surprise and chagrin, she would have none of it: her father, a distinguished railway executive, had told her all about the Sonnets. Bad as this was, worse was to come.

We have seen that that cautious scholar, Professor F.P.Wilson, regarded Leslie Hotson's conjectures about Shakespeare as the 'mare's nests' they were. Hotson's is a sad case, for he had a good nose for research, and then spoiled it practically all with his wild interpretations, really off the rails. I knew him a little, in fact we shared the same research assistant, Miss N.McN.O'Neill, at the Public Record Office. Early on I ventured to suggest that he might give us a collective portrait of all the theatre people who would have known Shakespeare: colleagues in the Lord Chamberlain's Company, fellow actors in it and writers for it. That would have been something substantial, real and factual – good background to Shakespeare.

Not a bit of it: he wasn't interested. He always wanted to take up something problematical and propose some 'solution' to it. I know no one whose judgment in these matters was so erratic – this is putting it mildly, and was quite well known; in fact it was so ludicrously off the rails as to be half-cracked. (He *was* an eccentric.) His book, *Shakespeare's Sonnets Dated*, has no idea of dating whatever: he was no historian. He did not see that the traditional dating of them to 1591/2 to 1594 was quite right. All is perfectly clear: no need for any confusion whatever. Hotson simply takes one Sonnet out of context, Sonnet 107 –

> The mortal moon hath her eclipse endured –

and supposes that this refers to the Spanish Armada, when everyone knows that 'the mortal moon' regularly refers to the Queen! Hotson produced a whole book dating the Sonnets back to the Armada of 1588, before Shakespeare began writing! All rubbish, wasting paper and print, and – what is worse – confusing people's minds, making nonsense of the subject.

As again with the famous misprint in *Henry V* about Falstaff on his death-bed: 'for his nose was as sharp as a pen, and *a table* of green fields'. The traditional emendation of this is ''*a babbled* of green fields'. Professor C.J.Sisson, most reliable of textual scholars, discusses this, and thinks it probable that Shakespeare wrote simply ''*a talked* of green fields'. Anyone familiar with Elizabethan handwriting would recognise that this is the probable reading. Sisson is in favour of keeping 'babbled' because it has established itself with time, and either 'talked' or 'babbled' will do equally well.

Not for Hotson, however. He has a ludicrous essay about its referring to a picture of green fields, i.e. of Grenville's! He refers to my biography of Grenville, where I merely mention that the Spaniards called him 'Campo Verde'. I think that the traditional pronunciation of the name was 'Grenfell'. What has any of this to do with it? Hotson is off the rails again – how to account for such crazy judgments?

Or take a later book of his, *Shakespeare by Hilliard: A Portrait Deciphered*. The portrait is the famous miniature of 'An Unknown Man Clasping a Hand Issuing from a Cloud.' Hotson would have us believe that this is an unrecognised portrait of Shakespeare. It is visibly nothing of the sort. We know exactly what he looked like from the Droeshout frontispiece to the First Folio. Have you ever seen a nobler dome of a cranium than on that head? Very large luminous eyes that take in everything; a big sexy nose, voluptuous lips, rather bald – there is a reference to that in the Sonnets; then the hairless, mobile cheeks of an actor. It is a recognisably convincing portrait of the man.

Quite unlike Hilliard's portrait of the Unknown Man: a differently shaped oval head, bearded, with notably small eyes and small shapely nose, curly hair. Couldn't Hotson *see*? Apparently not. He followed this up with his 'discovery' of who Mr W.H. was – all based on the common misconception that he was Shakespeare's young man *inside* the Sonnets. We were informed that this was a William Hatcliffe, a 'Prince of Purpoole' in some revels at an inn of court.

No one in the wide world fell for this nonsense – except Dame Veronica Wedgwood, who fell flat into the mare's nest. This was worse than personally disappointing: it was contrary to common sense. It corroborated G.M. Trevelyan's word to me: 'you and I know that Veronica is an historian of the second rank'.

We do not need to waste further time on Hotson's mare's nests: a whole book on 'theatre in the round', for example. Nobody thinks that Elizabethan plays were performed like that: we know enough about what Elizabethan playhouses and stages looked like, for all the controversy about details. A purely formal writ of attachment turned up in which one William Wayte craved surety of the peace against William Shakespeare, Francis Langley and a couple of others in November 1596. Nothing eventuated from it: it was simply formal evidence of a dispute, in which we find Shakespeare in association with Langley, at that time proprietor of the Swan Theatre (of the stage of which we have a detailed drawing by the way).

That is all there is to it. But Hotson, finding that Wayte was associated with a rumbustious Justice of the Peace in Surrey, one William Gardner, jumped to the conclusion that here we have the original of Justice Shallow. No evidence whatever – nor was the pushing Gardner a bit like the peaceable doting old Shallow in his Cotswold garden. Yet a further fat book, beautifully produced by the Nonesuch Press, was wasted on this mare's nest.

To do Hotson justice, his eagerness to find something new about Shakespeare and his nose for research turned up interesting information, if irrelevant to the subject. One search, however, was relevant. He followed up the lead in Shakespeare's will given by the reference to Sir Thomas Russell of Strensham as an executor. This was worth while – and in keeping with my early suggestion to him for information about people who knew Shakespeare. This had relevance, for Russell had property out at Alderminster, along the road into Stratford, and it showed the successful townsman who had made money from the theatre, on friendly terms with the local gentry. That is correct.

I must also do justice to Professor Terence Spencer, who came round from his earlier questioning to become quite friendly. He wrote a warm review of my *Christopher Marlowe*, which Professor G.B.Harrison, who knew about the Elizabethan age, described as 'the best biography' of him. (It has never yet reached the elevated status of academic syllabuses.) Spencer wrote in the end: 'Dr Rowse has done what nobody else has been able to do. He has created for the general reader pictures of Shakespeare of Stratford-upon-Avon and Marlowe of Canterbury as authors, living in a particular epoch and expressing in their writings their different personalities and social interests. This is important. For Shakespeare has been absurdly surrounded with a "mystery", which has spread a spurious kind of doubt and suspicion in the minds of some members of the public. Dr Rowse's books on Shakespeare and Marlowe are the popular answer, and we can applaud their wide circulation.'

Hence the necessity for aggression: to clear nonsense off the field, if possible. Not even this is over-generous: 'popular' is not the word for the leading scholar on the Elizabethan age. Spencer quoted (my favourite) Dr Johnson that a work may be corrected in details by 'minds incapable of achieving the whole work' – an admission much to the point. Actually I welcome any correction of fact, though *not one has been forthcoming*.

I know as well as the next man that it is not the conventional thing to express confidence: one is supposed to leave that to others. But since they do not speak up, I am forced to do so myself. That this is necessary is evident from a *Times* review of my edition of the Sonnets: 'it is highly improbable that there will ever be certainty about the young man and the rival poet any more than over the Dark Lady'. One simply has to put one's foot down about facts.

Not that my Oxford friends were much help. Here was the poet Auden, in a BBC broadcast, referring to Southampton's 'exclusive interest in women'! When everybody knows that the young man was bisexual. Wystan corrected the howler when he republished the broadcast, but no invitation has ever been forthcoming from the BBC to learn the facts of the matter from the leading authority on it – which Wystan certainly was not.

Professor Trevor-Roper was a young friend – if I were not so cautious I might dare even to think of him as an early *protégé*. When he was *very* young he had written an article doubting whether Shakespeare had written his own works – the last infirmity of a noble (or ennobled) mind. He has recovered from that error of judgment since. But when I was in trouble with the conventional academics, he weighed in against me about the Sonnets and Mr W.H. Surprisingly, he repeated the mistake that 'the only begetter' meant the inspirer of the Sonnets – when this rested upon the misapprehension that W.H. was Shakespeare's man, when he was not.

I had explained how it was that Thorp was wishing Harvey 'all happiness and that eternity promised by our ever-living poet' – i.e. the eternity Shakespeare had promised Southampton if he would only marry and carry on the family to posterity. This was what Thorp was wishing young Harvey now; for in 1607 his elderly wife, Southampton's mother, died, leaving him all the household goods and chattels; in 1608 he married a young wife; this is why in 1609 Thorp is wishing him all happiness, and the prospect of having progeny for posterity. QED.

It was all clear, for the first time: why did not pupil and *protégé* take note of what their former tutor had to tell them? I refrain from noting that my distinguished *protégé* has made other misjudgments since – and mistakes should be corrected. I am very willing to correct any of mine, if and when specified. Why were they so keen to contradict me – and get it wrong?

In all this *fracas* a New York publisher, Robert Giroux, came out with a book on the Sonnets which did better than these Oxford professionals. He tells us that he approached the subject 'as a book publisher and an amateur'. But he saw clearly that the patron was the person for whom and to whom the Sonnets were written, and dismissed all the William Haughtons, William Hatcliffes William Hugheses (Oscar Wilde's blithe boy) that mixed-up people thought of as Shakespeare's.

Mr Giroux doubted one point that I had made – that Southampton had written to Emilia on Shakespeare's behalf, and she, naturally enough, had taken the opportunity to entangle the young Earl, a more promising proposition than an impecunious player with wife and family in the country. But this as we have seen is precisely what happened:

> He learned but surety-like to write for me
> Under that bond that him as fast doth bind.

Mr Giroux would not know that this was the regular convention in the Elizabethan age.

One does not blame a modern publisher for not appreciating this – especially in that Mr Giroux, as a publisher, spotted something else that was significant. The only remaining problem about the Sonnets is why they were not reprinted until years had passed, and both Shakespeare and Southampton were long dead. Mr Giroux's suggestion that someone must have stepped in and stopped re-publication is only a conjecture, but in this instance a highly probable one.

We may be sure that Shakespeare had nothing to do with the publication in 1609: that was the publisher's doing, grateful to Harvey as the only one who had got the manuscript for him. We know that Southampton was not pleased by his mother's marrying young William Harvey; we are not told what he thought about her leaving him all the household goods and chattels. But in 1609 Southampton was now a public figure, high up in government; Shakespeare, the foremost of playwrights, very much bent on being the gentleman.

Neither of them can have relished having the story of their relations exposed to public view.

No sonnets have ever been more autobiographical, nearer the bone, than these – and yet there have not been wanting numbskulls to treat them as 'literary exercises'! We have reason to be grateful to this publisher for bringing out a likelihood that no one had thought of.

Nor had anyone ever realised the significance of the fact that, in writing the Sonnets, Shakespeare was the only one of the Elizabethan dramatists to write an autobiography. It took me some time to realise how autobiographical a writer he was, and years before I spotted and worked out the entirely autobiographical inspiration of *The Two Gentlemen of Verona*: the rivalry of the two friends for the same woman, one of them betraying the other, then the other making way for the betrayer – most unconvincingly, according to all the critics without a clue. All this corroborated from, and in the very language of, the Sonnets, dating and all. No wonder nobody had ever found a 'source' for the play.

All this supports an original consideration. Naturally the auto-biographical is to the fore in Shakespeare's early work – what else was there to go on, except for his reading? His experience as a countryman, fond of sport, was something to go on – and it is all there; so too with his reading in the classics, from schooldays and a stint as usher in the country. It was not much – compared with Marlowe, for instance: he had to make the most of it, and was a great one for making the most of a little. Then came the overwhelming experience of London, admission into the aristocratic circle of his patron, the Lord Chamberlain's Company, the Lord Chamberlain's discarded young mistress, and all.

Here was an important clue to follow throughout his work. I had from the first realised the true nature of *Love's Labour's Lost*, as a skit on the Southampton circle by its poet; the occasion of *A Mid-summer Night's Dream* being that of the Countess's second marriage on 2 May 1594; the inspiration of *Romeo and Juliet* in the murderous feud of Southampton's closest friends, the Danvers brothers, down in his neighbourhood; the many reflections of his admired leader Essex. And so on.

These tell-tale traces and others all through his work, when put together with Notes to elucidate them, made a useful little manual: *Shakespeare's Self-Portrait: Passages from his Work*. It is not yet required reading in schools – though it tells you more than heaps of dead commentary: it is Shakespeare himself to the life.

I dedicated it to President Reagan 'for his historic honour to Shakespeare's Profession'. After all, he is the only actor to achieve such an eminence. Proud of his experience as an actor and, for all the pressures of politics, he has kept contact with the theatre. He wrote to me that, like Richard Burton, he had performed Petruchio in *The Taming of the Shrew*, and expressed good wishes for making the plays more 'accessible' with *The Contemporary Shakespeare*.

The book was dismissed with a supercilious sentence in a typical *Times Literary Supplement* 'review', by a Professor Inga-Stina Ewbank. All that this 'expert' had to say about the book was to question the dedication: 'is he being ironic, and what exactly does he mean? With Flamineo, I am in a mist.' How absurd, it means simply what it says – and it is always best for simpletons to take things simply and directly. She had nothing to learn from the book – she devoted the resources of her intellect to 'the often brilliant arguments of *The Devil's Party: Critical Counter-Interpretations of Shakespearean Drama* which help to clear many a mist'. (Mist seems to favour this mind, a Scotch-Swedish mist, I take it.) Professor Inga-Stina Ewbank was more impressed by works on 'Shakespeare and the Author-Function', and 'Disrupting Sexual Difference: Meaning and Gender in the Comedies'. We learn that 'the problem is, I think, that "text-centred" may become so issue-centred that not only performance but the actual words of the text are brushed aside. In *Patriarchal Structures* Erickson is intent on finding unease about genders in *Antony and Cleopatra* ... Cleopatra's apotheosis explicitly converts the maternal image from life-giving nurturance into "an easy way to die".'

This, according to Professor Ewbank, 'no doubt inadvertently weakens the naturalistic image of a mother asking for peace and quiet not only for the sake of her suckling baby but also so as to be able herself to give in to the irresistible drowsiness which comes with nursing. The quality of felt life in this fictive situation would seem to tell a great deal more about Cleopatra's first-hand experience of motherhood than about her "misusing" the maternal image.'

Pope has a thought on such critics which is much to the point:

> Who explain a thing till all men doubt it,
> And write about it, and still write about it . . .
> Sinking from thought to thought, a vast profound,
> Plunged for her sense, but found no bottom there.

Can you recognise Cleopatra, in this academic waffle? There ought to be a close season for such people writing about Shakespeare.

One should not perhaps lecture professors, though they ask for it. One may, however, apply a remark of a better writer, Saki: 'One might as well lecture a mole on colour-blindness.' And for the organ in which such stuff appeared, Pope again has a word:

> All nonsense thus, of old or modern date,
> Shall in thee centre, from thee circulate.

However, Inga-Stina can approve of one Gary Taylor, 'whose description of *his experience* [!] of Cleopatra's death says more in two pages about the play, if not about gender criticism'. Professor Ewbank was not in a mist about Gary Taylor, if she was about Shakespeare himself throughout my book. She should have read that: she would have learned something. Mr Gary Taylor was one of the editors of the new Oxford Shakespeare, who put up a show about 'discovering' a piece of madrigal verse, 'Shall I die?', with which to adorn its pages as if it were Shakespeare's. It was exposed in columns of superfluous comment for what it is: a conventional piece of madrigal verse of which there are many comparable examples. If the reader looks up *The Oxford Book of Madrigal Verse* he will find a dozen such, and half-a-dozen with similar opening lines.

There were only two exceptions to this chorus of condemnation: Professor Schoenbaum gave it his enthusiastic imprimatur; Mr Stanley Wells, Taylor's fellow-editor, was more circumspect, he gave it his approval, if rather negatively. I fancy, however, that this third-rate poem appears in the new Oxford Shakespeare as if it were his! The 'discovery' of this blameless piece was arrived at with the aid of computers. When asked for my opinion of the matter I said merely that no amount of computerising could compensate for the lack of literary judgment.

I had already been unfavourably impressed by Mr Taylor's edition of *Henry V*. An historical play needs an historical approach. So far from understanding the background, and indeed the content, of the play Mr Taylor is antipathetic to it and anachronistically modern. 'No one bored by war will be interested in *Henry V*', he informs us. What an approach! '*Henry V* alone wholly dedicates itself to dramatising this brutal, exhilarating and depressingly persistent activity.' One may deplore war without obtruding a twentieth-century view of the subject upon a sixteenth-century work. He finds the war-crisis of 1598–9, at the back of the play and in its whole atmosphere, 'a rather unseemly and ridiculous fervour'. He does not know what he is talking about: it was in fact the most dangerous crisis in the long Elizabethan struggle over Ireland.

Nor does he know what kind of man Henry V was: 'because he did not know how to govern his own kingdom, he determined to make war upon his neighbours'. Historians know that Henry V was one of the ablest of all medieval rulers. K.B.McFarlane at Oxford, who knew more about the period than anyone else, declared that all in all Henry V was the greatest of our kings. It is hardly worth while going further with anyone so ignorant. Mr Taylor has a glimmer that Shakespeare's audience might have been interested – trust Shakespeare to know! – in the arguments justifying Henry's claim to the French throne: '*as we are not*, and listening to long and intellectually complex sermons (*as we are not*)'. Such anachronistic opinions are a disqualification for the editor of an historical play.

'Such dynastic justifications of military conquest seem to us wholly trumped up and chimerical.' Anachronistic again, and bad historical judgment, for in fact they were not so to the men of the time, either in England or in France. 'We expect from archbishops (in the theatre at least) either bland vacuousness or theological contortions.' This is not true, even today: witness Archbishop Becket's arguments that occupy much of Eliot's *Murder in the Cathedral*.

From such a source we are not surprised to hear that interest in the author of the plays is regarded as 'quietly satisfying an idle biographical curiosity'. I welcome this give-away, for it bears out my view that such superciliousness is apt to go with intellectual inferiority. And I fear that such treatment of an historical play, when so much of Shakespeare's work is historical, hardly bodes well for the Oxford Shakespeare. Did we in fact need it?

I do not think that we need any more ordinary editions at all –

we have plenty of them already to choose from. I recommend, for a collected edition of all the works in one volume, that of Professor C.J.Sisson; for the reason I have given – that, of all Shakespeare scholars, he was the one most familiar with Elizabethan language, from the documents illustrating everyday life, not only from literary sources. That is what best appeals to an historian, who knows its necessity, especially in interpreting the dialogue in the plays. This should be supplemented, for dealing with many obscurities and difficulties in the text, with his *New Readings in Shakespeare* (2 vols). I found this indispensable in working at *The Contemporary Shakespeare*.

From the account I have had to give in this book of the obtuseness and obstruction with which all the new information, the findings and discoveries, have been regarded, I never expected that *The Contemporary Shakespeare* would be welcomed by these people. That did not deter me: never pay any attention to the opinions of the third-rate, or set oneself to satisfy *their* standards! As a successful contemporary dramatist, Arthur Miller, found: 'if I had listened to the Critics I'd have died drunk in the gutter'. That was *à propos* of his *Death of a Salesman* which, damned by the critics, became a modern classic, successful across the world in many languages.

I calculated that it would not be the theatre people, at least in the United States, who would be chiefly obtuse: they would be more open-minded, some of them ready to experiment. Not as yet in Britain. That too I expected, for my opinion of our society today must be fairly well known – the demotic confusion, absence of standards, no sense of quality. As another Fellow of All Souls says, with Equality the first thing that goes is Quality.

The library assistant who thought that I had no sense of Shakespeare's verse also thought that, in modernising, I had in some respects gone too far, and in others, not far enough. A fair-minded person would judge from that that I had struck a happy medium. My own opinion is that perhaps I have not gone far enough, been too conservative, in accordance with my (reactionary) temperament. (I *am* a reactionary, but an open-minded one.)

One must always give reasons, rational reasons, not follow one's prejudices. One leading lady in Washington, highly intelligent and modern-minded, said that she fancied the flavouring of 'thou's' and 'thee's'. Personally, I do not; but that is not the reason for getting rid of them: the reason is that their use demands the second person singular in hundreds of verbs, all those 'st's'. We no longer use them: that is enough. Another, equally intelligent, New York lady would 'give her right arm to retain "quietus" in *Hamlet*'. Personally I would prefer to retain 'quietus': I know what it means, but most people do not.

This is the principle upon which I operate in general: when most people do not know what the word or phrase means then simplify. This is where I have been too conservative. The reason for this is that I am so used to Elizabethan words and usages that sometimes I have let them stand, without reflecting that other people might not know them. In one or two cases I have been reproved for this excessive conservatism. I accept this reproof. I do not accept the opposite one. One journalist reproved me for rendering 'a couch of luxury and damned incest' as 'a couch of lustfulness and damnèd incest'. He would not know that 'luxury' in Elizabethan usage meant lust; nor would he notice that 'lustfulness' has the equivalent three syllables, while 'damnèd' is given the proper accent by me. I take no notice of such people's opinions: it is for them to learn.

All I wish is Openmindedness: it should be obvious to all that that is the only right and proper attitude. Open-minded myself, I am open to consider alternative suggestions or to have second thoughts. Take the famous line in *Hamlet* when the Ghost, his father, says that he was cut off

> Unhouseled, disappointed, unaneled.

We may be sure that moderns will not know the meaning of any of those words, so they must be changed. 'Unhouseled' means not having received the sacrament; 'disappointed' means unappointed, unprepared; 'unaneled' means without having received extreme unction. I have rendered this,

> Unconfessed, unready, unanointed.

I think I should prefer now something like

> Unshriven, unanointed, unprepared –

that ends more strongly on the accented syllable as the original does.

'Unhouseled' really means uncommunicated. In Catholic rites we still have a 'houseling cloth' at the communion to catch anything of the sacred elements that falls. They would not know that. It is something, if one is to understand the Elizabethan age, to have been brought up an Anglican. And – here is a relevant point – it is obvious from all through his work that Shakespeare's sympathies were that way, decidedly not Puritan. Southampton, as we have seen, was a Roman Catholic, until he sensibly 'verted with James I's accession.

I have even, in one or two instances, been so conservative as to reinstate, with Sisson, an original Elizabethan usage which eighteenth- and nineteenth-century editors had displaced, when it is clear enough to us moderns. The seventeenth and eighteenth century had no compunction in re-writing and altering Shakespeare, giving tragedies happy endings, and so on. Dryden suggested modernising Donne – as Pope did some of the Satires, and my friend Coghill did Chaucer. Nothing of that in this historian's *Contemporary Shakespeare*. Yet, instead of explaining to the public what this edition does for them, what the intention is, the typical media-men of a squalid age can talk about my 'translating' Shakespeare – how ignorant, as if into a foreign language; or 'rewriting' him as Dryden and others did. Heaven forbid! – no historian would wish for that.

No mention, of course, of what may be learned from the Introductions, which I set most store by. For several of these contain new information illuminating the play, not only its circumstances but its character and content, such as only an experienced Elizabethan historian could contribute. This is true not only for *The Two Gentlemen of Verona*, *Love's Labour's Lost*, *A Midsummer Night's Dream*, and *Romeo and Juliet*, which all have Southampton associations; but also for *Troilus and Cressida*, *All's Well that Ends Well*, *Cymbeline* and finally *Henry VIII*.

A typical dismissal in the *Times Literary Supplement* describes the project as 'finally reductive' – whatever that cliché means. 'It turns the plays into mere receptacles of conventional wisdom, dilapidated portrait galleries in which history is annihilated in the interests of a shoddy and stunted psychology rarely rise above the level of the mottoes in a Christmas cracker.' This outburst is by one Terence Hawkes. I do not know who this great authority is, or what he has achieved, never having heard of him. It all helps to corroborate my view of the decline of standards in the shoddy society, and its media, today.

The *Times Educational Supplement*, in the person of one Ralph Berry (ever heard of his achievements either?) goes so far as to say that 'the call for a fully modernised Shakespeare is periodically raised, and with reason'. It then concludes, says this authority with an *ipse dixit*, 'but Rowse's is not the answer'.

Professor Robert Kirsch wondered how many more hundreds of years we should have to wait before the right combination of scholarship and intuition would have brought the Dark Lady to light. I take leave to say that, whatever the jaundiced may say about *The Contemporary Shakespeare*, the public will have to wait a long while before there is a better, or more helpful to the reader.

Index

Admiral's Company, Lord, 75, 96
Alderminster, 161
Allen, Avis, 8
Alleyn, Edward, 75
America, US, 10, 33, 57, 92, 115, 130, 168
America, Modern Language Association, 24–5
American Bar Association, 28
Anikst, Alexandr, 98
Appeasement, 155, 156, 158
Arden family, 78–9; Forest of, 78; Mary, 71
Armada of 1588, 21, 159; of 1596, 90
Astrology, 38–9
Aubrey, John, 1, 74, 103
Auchincloss, Louis, 57–8, 157
Auden, W.H., 35, 36, 162
Azores, 10, 43

Bacon, Delia, 29
Bacon, Francis, 15, 17, 66, 88
Bakeless, John, 28
Baldwin, T.W., 9
Bancroft, Richard, 45
Barcheston, 95
Bassano, Baptista, 7, 43; Emilia, Mrs Lanier, 7, 39–42, 43–55, 66–7, 75, 156, 163
Bath, 39
Beckett, Samuel, 36

Beeching, Dean, 41
Bellot couple, betrothed by Shakespeare, 99, 120
Betjeman, John, 147
Bevin, Ernest, 147
Blackfriars, 44, 103, 121
Boleyn, Anne, 12, 100
Books: Annotated Shakespeare, 127–8; Bosworth Field and the Wars of the Roses, 89; Christopher Marlowe: A Biography, 77; Contemporary Shakespeare, 129–45, 168; Court and Country: Studies in Tudor Social History, 12; Elizabethan Age, 7, 37; Prefaces to Shakespeare's Plays, 128; Ralegh and the Throckmortons, 11; Shakespeare's Self-Portrait, 165; Shakespeare's Sonnets: A Modern Edition, 30–1; William Shakespeare: A Biography, 29–31
Bowers, Fredson, 135
Bradbrook, M.C., 68
Brecht, B., 123
Bridges, Robert, 38
Brighton Arts Festival, 34
Brooke, Arthur, 74
Brooks, Cleanth, 18
Brown, Ivor, 148
Burbage, Richard, 26
Burgess, Anthony, 58
Burghley, Lord, 86

Burton, Richard, 133–4, 165
Butler, Samuel, 17
Buxton, John, 8, 55

Cadiz, 76
Cambridge, 35, 71, 102
Cambridge School of Eng. Lit., 35–6
Cambridge Shakespeare, the, 27, 149–50
Canterbury, 10, 77
Carey, William, 44; and v. Hunsdon
Carnsew, William, 12
Carpenter, H., 35
Carr, Robert, earl of Somerset, 43, 112
Cecil, Lord David, 15, 158
Cecil, Robert, earl of Salisbury, 20, 86, 88
Chamberlain's Company, Lord, 64, 75, 105, 111, 159
Chambers' Biographical Dictionary, 5
Chambers, E.K., 7–8, 27–8, 39, 69, 72, 91–2, 117
Charlecote, 71
Chaucer, Geoffrey, 7, 123
Chettle, Henry, 70
Christie, Agatha, 6, 113
Churchill, W.S., 156
Clifford, Lady Anne, 48, 50
Cobham, 7th and 8th Lords, 103
Coghill, Nevill, 5, 7, 55
Connolly, Cyril, 147–8
Cook, A.J., 97–8
Cookham, 49, 50
Cooper, William, 140
Corkine, William, 77
Cotswolds, 71, 121
Coventry, 95
Criticism, literary, 61
Crow, John, 33, 150
Cumberland, Margaret, countess, 48–50

Daniel, Samuel, 47–8, 52
Danvers, Sir Charles, 73; Sir Henry, 73; Lady, 74
Daventry, 95
Doran, Madeleine, 153
Dover, 112
Drayton, Michael, 52
Droeshout portrait of Shakespeare, 160
Dryden, John, 170

Duff Cooper, 127

Edmonds, Piers, 108
Egremont, Lord, 155
Eliot, T.S., 36, 123, 167
Elizabeth I, 12, 18, 21, 72, 75, 82, 85, 86–7, 88, 100, 107–8, 109, 144, 159
Elizabethan Age, 3, 4, 61, 163
Empson, William, 153–4
Erasmus, 33
Erastus, 33
Essex, Robert Devereux, 2nd earl, 21, 23, 66, 82, 84–5, 87–8, 105, 108
Eton College, 147
Evans, G.B., 57, 129, 156
Ewbank, I.-S., 165–6

Fastolf, Sir John, 94
Feminism, 51–4
Field, Richard, Stratford man, prints Shakespeare's poems, 44, 66, 121
Fisher, Sidney T., 150–1
Fitton, Mary, 5–6, 15, 148
Fletcher, John, 123–4
Florio, John, 48, 53, 67, 74, 122
Folger Shakespeare Library, 25, 57–8, 139, 156
Forman, Simon, 7, 8, 37–9, 42–5, 99, 121
France, 21, 23, 66, 107
Fripp, E.I., 91

Gardner, Helen, 55–6
Gardner, William, 161
Garnet, Henry, 112
Gielgud, Sir John, 32, 138, 145
Gilbert, Adrian, 10
Giroux, Robert, 163
Globe Theatre, 39, 86, 96, 121
Gower, John, 119
Greg, Sir Walter, 135
Greene, Robert, 69–70, 121
Grenville, Sir Richard, 10, 160
Gunpowder Plot, 110

Hakluyt, Richard, 101
Halliwell-Phillips, J.O., 37
Harington, Sir John, 12
Harvard University, 57, 97, 129, 156
Harvey, Dr William, 1–2

Harvey, Sir William, i.e. 'Mr W.H.', 53, 92, 163
Hazlitt, William, 92
Heneage, Sir Thomas, 15, 72–3
Henri IV, also as Navarre, 21, 64, 73, 90
Henry V, 93–4, 167
Henry VII, 120
Henry VIII, 44, 99–100
Herbert, William, Lord, 15, 27; v. also Pembroke
Hesketh, Lady, 11
Hilliard, Nicholas, 160
Hitler, A., 155
Hobbes, Thomas, 1
Hoby, Margaret, Lady, 7, 39
Hoffman, Calvin B., 28, 57
Holinshed's Chronicles, 80, 110
Homosexuality, 17, 19, 66, 78
Hotson, Leslie, 4, 21, 77–8, 104, 159–61
Housman, A.E., 16, 35
Howard, Frances, countess of Hertford, 43
Howard, Frances, countess of Somerset, 43
Howard, Frances, duchess of Richmond and Lennox, 42–3
Howard, Lord Henry, 89; as Northampton, 112
Hunsdon, George, 2nd Lord, patron of Forman, 7, 39
Hunsdon, Henry, 1st Lord, Lord Chamberlain, patron of Shakespeare's Company, and of Emilia Bassano, 7, 39, 43–4, 104

Illinois, University of, 9, 57
Ireland, 82–4, 107
Isaacs, J., 153
Italy, 74, 126

Jacobean age, 118
James, Henry, 5
James I, 43, 99, 100–1, 109, 110–12, 120–1
Jay, Douglas, 120
Jesuits, 21–2, 112
Jews, 53, 75, 122
Johnson, Dr, 60, 100, 111, 116

Jonson, Ben, 2, 3, 12, 78, 81, 103, 104–5

Kenilworth, 72
Kent, Susan, countess, 44, 48
'King's Evil', 111
Kirsch, Robert, 9, 171
Knight, Wilson, 35, 152

La Rochefoucauld, F. de, 147
Lambarde, William, 86–7
Lanier, Alphonse, 43–5, 48; and v. Bassano
Lecky, W.E.H., 34
Leicester, Robert Dudley, earl, 72
Levin, Bernard, 150
Lewis, C.S., 35, 55
Lincoln, Abraham, 156
London, 8, 46, 56, 76, 78, 85, 86, 98, 126, 150
Long, Henry, 73
Lopez, Dr, 21, 53, 75
Lothian, Lord, 155
Lowell, Robert, xi
Lucy, Sir William, 71
Luny (or Loony), Professor, 29
Lynchburg College, Virginia, 133

Macaulay, Lord, 11
McFarlane, K.B., 81, 167
McGill university, xi, 56
MacLennan, Hugh, xi
McManaway, J. G., 25, 57, 140
Macmillan, Harold, ix
Madrid, 10
Malone, Edmund, 15
Mamoulian, Rouben, 135–6
Marlowe, Christopher, x, 17, 20–1, 28, 74, 75, 76–8, 102, 152
Maurois, André, 32
Meres, Francis, 76
Milford Haven, 120
Miller, Arthur, 61, 168
Milton, John, 51, 123
Montaigne, M., 122
Moon, Sir Penderel, 17, 30
More, Sir Thomas, 89
Morison, S. E., 56
Morley, Thomas, 104
Mortimer, Raymond, 147

Mountjoy (Montjoie) household, 98–9, 103

Muggeridge, Malcolm, 61, 148

Muir, Kenneth, 35, 147

Netherlands, 82

New York, 158, 163; Metropolitan Museum, 127; Pierpont Morgan Library, 32–3; 'Today Show', 133–4, 135

Normandy, 23–4, 60

Northamptonshire, 11

Oman, Sir Charles, 144

O'Neil, Hugh, 84

Orwell, George, 115–16

Ostend, 86

Oxford, 5, 18, 25, 33, 37, 55, 71–2, 112, 158; Bodleian Library, 7, 9, 37–9, 47, 55, 56; Colleges: All Souls, 4, 17, 30, 33, 35, 56, 155, 168; Balliol, 33; Christ Church, 33, 34, 56; Magdalen, 37; Worcester, 5; Eng. Lit. School, 4, 33–4, 35, 55–6, 140; History School, xi, 33–4

Oxford, Edward de Vere, 17th earl, 17, 28–9, 94

Oxford Shakespeare, the, 166–7

Papp, Joseph, 133

Paris, 117

Parsons, Robert, 22

Paulerspury, 11

Pembroke, William Herbert, 3rd earl, 26–7, 111, 148; Mary, countess, 47, 48, 49

Penheale, Cornwall, 10

Pérez, Antonio, 65–6, 75

Philadelphia, 29

Physicians, Royal College, 38, 107

Plague, 68–9, 74–5, 119

Poor Law, 115

Pope, Alexander, 61, 103, 166, 170

Prior, Roger, xi–xii, 8, 12, 47, 75, 120, 156

Public Record Office, London, 9–10, 12, 35, 159

Quennell, Peter, 33–4

Quiller-Couch, A.T., 28, 126

Ralegh, Sir Walter, 10, 12, 20, 70, 147

Reagan, President R., 115, 165

Rheims, 77

Rich, Lord, 61

Richard III, 89, 93

Ricks, Christopher, 154

Riverside Shakespeare, the, 57

Roosevelt, President F.D., 116

Russell, Sir Thomas, 161

Russia, Soviet, 36, 98, 115–16, 122

Sainte-Beuve, C.A., xi, 59

'Saki', 166

Sartre, J.P., 36

Schiller, F., 152

Schoenbaum, S., 154, 166

Scotland, 82–3, 109, 110, 121

Scott, Sir Walter, 80

Shakespeare establishment, x, 25–6, 34, 55–8, 60, 146

Shakespeare, Hamnet, 91; John, 78

Shakespeare, William, as Berowne, 64–5; *Plays: All's Well That Ends Well*, 107–8; *Antony and Cleopatra*, 112–13, 124; *As You Like It*, 76–8; *Coriolanus*, 113–14, 117; *Cymbeline*, 120–1; *Hamlet*, 61, 85–6, 105, 136, 169–70; *1 and 2 Henry IV*, 92–5; *Henry V*, 95–6, 159–60, 166–7; *1, 2, 3 Henry VI*, 60, 85–6, 105, 136, 169–70; *Henry VIII*, 99–100; *Julius Caesar*, 106–7; *King John*, 90–1; *King Lear*, 112; *Love's Labour's Lost*, 4, 64–9, 111–12, 113; *Macbeth*, 83, 110–12; *Measure for Measure*, 109; *The Merchant of Venice*, 53, 58, 75–6; *The Merry Wives of Windsor*, 103; *A Midsummer Night's Dream*, 71–3, 125, 153; *Much Ado About Nothing*, 85, 102–3; *Othello*, 58, 110; *Pericles*, 118–20; *Richard II*, 83, 84–5; *Richard III*, 88–9; *Romeo and Juliet*, 73–5; *The Taming of the Shrew*, 71, 133–4; *The Tempest*, 60, 121–3; *Timon of Athens*, 117–18; *Titus Andronicus*, 81; *Troilus and Cressida*, 87–8, 104–6; *Twelfth Night*, 103–4; *The Two Gentlemen of Verona*, 58, 61–4, 164; *The Two Noble Kinsmen*, 123–6; *The Winter's*

Tale, 121; *Poems*, 16, 19, 24, 53; *Sonnets*, 4, 6, 15–31, 40–2, 53, 152, 162, 164
Shaw, Bernard, 80, 108, 123
Shirley brothers, 104
Sidney, Sir Philip, 61
Smith, D. Mack, 56
Snobbery, 29
Snow, C.P., 32
Southampton, Henry Wriothesley, 2nd earl, 23; Henry Wriothesley, 3rd earl (Shakespeare's), 2, 6, 17–19, 22–4, 43, 46, 54, 66, 71, 73, 107–8, 111–12, 122, 162, 163; Elizabeth, wife, 18, 107; Mary, mother, 15, 72, 108, 153, 162
Southwark Cathedral, 119–20
Spain, 82, 99–100
Speaight, Robert, 104
Spencer, Terence, 151–3, 161–2
Spender, Stephen, 106
Stewart, J.I.M., 32, 56, 146
Stopes, C.C., 92
Stratford, 26, 70, 71, 91, 95, 112, 114, 161
Sutton Coldfield, 95
Swift, Jonathan, 156
Sykes, Christopher, 150

Taylor, Gary, 166–7
Thomson, James, 153
Thornborough, John, 37
Thorp, Thomas, 9, 53, 162
Throckmorton, Sir Arthur, 10–11
Times, the, 149, 151, 155, 162; *Educational Supplement*, 170–1; *Literary Supplement*, xii, 33, 34, 68, 135, 149, 150, 155, 165, 170

Titchfield, 73
Tolstoy, L., 123
Topcliffe, Richard, 12
Trevelyan, G.M., 56, 160
Trevor-Roper, H.R., 162–3
Twine, Lawrence, 119

Venice, 58, 76, 126
Vidal, Gore, 92, 115
Virginia, 60, 101, 118, 121–2
Virginia Company, 54

Wallace, C.W., 98
Warwick Castle, 89
Warwickshire, 14, 71, 78, 92, 114, 126
Washington, DC, 25, 168
Wayte, William, 160–1
Wedgwood, C.V., 158–9, 160, 163
Wells, Stanley, 166
Welsh, the, 83
Westminster, 45, 47; Abbey, 43, 93
Wickham, Glynne, 99
Wilde, Oscar, 17, 36
Wilkins, George, 120
Williamson, J.A., 10
Wilmcote, 78
Wilson, F.P., 4, 102, 146, 159
Wilson, J. Dover, 26–7, 28, 39, 86, 95, 148–9
Wilton House, 111
Wiltshire, 73
Wolfit, Donald, 32
Wright, Louis B., 57
Wyeth, Andrew, 131

Yates, Frances, 68
Yeats, W.B., 123